POWER,

RIGHTS,

AND POVERTY:

CONCEPTS AND CONNECTIONS

Power, Rights, and Poverty: Concepts and Connections

Edited by
Ruth Alsop

ISBN-10: 0-8213-6310-7   ISBN-13: 978-0-8213-6310-2
eISBN: 0-8213-6311-5
DOI: 10.1596/978-0-8213-6310-2

Contents

Foreword

This volume brings together background materials and discussions from a two-day working meeting on "Power, Rights, and Poverty Reduction" held jointly by the World Bank and the United Kingdom Department for International Development in March 2004. The meeting represented an important step in our continuing effort to understand issues of empowerment, power, and human rights, and how they influence and are influenced by our work.

While empowerment has been identified to be of instrumental value in contributing to developmental effectiveness, good governance, and growth, empowerment is equally of value intrinsically in improving people's lives. Whether it is a Brazilian woman gaining a mailing address and thereby having a better chance at securing a job, a Bolivian man acquiring an identity card and with it a right to vote, or urban slum dwellers in South Africa organizing to influence policymaking, these experiences remind us that, while there is still much ground to cover, enabling citizens to claim their positions as equal members of society can have an enormous impact on their lives.

Since the World Development Report 2000/2001: Attacking Poverty, empowerment has been increasingly addressed across many networks and sectors within the Bank. The Bank has clearly committed itself to working to empower poor people. However, for our work to be effective, there is further consolidation and substantive work to be done, and this working meeting was one way of building on experience to take forward these agendas.

An empowerment approach has direct relevance to rights-based approaches to development, which are based on a sense of justice and equity in relations between people, as well as the idea that individuals have a set of entitlements for which the state is responsible to advance, promote, and protect. But it's in the practice of poverty reduction that we really see the links and the differences. In researching the paper I helped prepare on poverty reduction strategies for a recent meeting in New York on Human Rights and Development, it became clear that much of the poverty work of the World Bank and other donors is informed by the same notions of equality and non-discrimination that are central to human rights and empowerment approaches to development. For example, the PRSP model seeks to increase accountability and transparency and to enhance citizen inclusion in policymaking and governance—all central features of both rights and empowerment approaches to development. The papers in this volume suggest strong conceptual affinities between rights and empowerment approaches to poverty alleviation. They also suggest that the two approaches overlap strongly but that in practice an empowerment approach is more likely to have the effect of reinforcing citizen rights rather than directly addressing them. The difference between PRSPs, which incorporate an empowerment approach to poverty reduction, and human rights approaches is that the former are operational strategies necessarily acknowledging resource constraints and seeking explicitly to deal with tradeoffs. Human rights approaches on the other hand, widely characterized as legitimate claims that give rise to correlative obligations or duties, focus more on the fulfillment of legal obligations of states to citizens.

Issues of empowerment, power, and rights are not simple ones to grasp, and must be addressed with care and thoughtfulness. We must begin by understanding what these concepts mean on the ground, and how our existing activities and tools can support their development. We offer this volume as an initial contribution to this effort, and hope that it will provoke broader discussions and action with the goal of improving the scale and success of our work. We welcome your reactions and contributions.

Gobind Nankani
Vice President
Poverty Reduction and Economic Management

Part I

Exploring Concepts and Applications:
Presenter Papers

1. Power, Rights, and Poverty Reduction

Ruth Alsop, Poverty Reduction Group, PREM, World Bank, and
Andrew Norton, Policy Unit, UK Department for International Development

Power and rights. These terms are increasingly heard in the corridors and offices of international development agencies, but the notions are less apparent in the poverty alleviation activities of such organizations. Recognizing this discrepancy, the World Bank and DFID co-sponsored a two-day meeting in Washington, DC, in March 2004, to enhance understanding of the relationships among power, rights, and poverty reduction and to use that understanding as the basis for a discussion about strategic objectives, foci, and content of work programs within the World Bank and DFID. The World Bank's Empowerment Team, located in the Poverty Reduction and Economic Management group, hosted the March meeting. Participants included representatives of the World Bank, DFID, and research and academic institutions. The objectives of the meeting were largely met: participants from DFID and the Bank left with a better understanding of the conceptual underpinnings and relationships among power, rights, and poverty reduction. While accepting the sensitivities and complexity of the subject matter, practical options for operationalizing work on these issues also became clearer during the meeting. Both organizations are currently moving these options forward individually and jointly.

From Ideas to Action

The papers in part I of this publication were prepared to inform the two days of discussion. Each was written by a leading thinker on power or rights, and each supported a session led by the author. The order of papers in this part reflects the role each played in moving the discussion from ideas to action. The first series of papers deals with definitions and concepts, illustrating these with country experiences. The second set of papers addresses topics that could be critical for agencies such as the World Bank and DFID to focus upon. Part II of this publication contains supplemental materials: a brief paper describing the World Bank Empowerment Team's approach to understanding

> "THE CENTRALITY OF POWER IS RARELY EXPLICITLY RECOGNIZED IN THE BANK'S LENDING AND ANALYTIC WORK."

and measuring empowerment, a paper summarizing the debate and outcomes of the meeting, a summary of the major conceptualizations of power, and a short literature overview.

The World Bank and DFID use the terms empowerment, power, and rights frequently. However, given that the centrality of power is rarely explicitly recognized in the Bank's lending and analytic work, the Empowerment Team wanted to draw on the knowledge of leading thinkers to clarify its understanding of the current discourse on power and rights, how they linked in theory and practice, and what the implications were in terms of the opportunities and limitations of addressing power and rights in the institutional context of the World Bank.

The Empowerment Team defines empowerment as increasing the capacity of individuals and groups to make choices and to transform these choices into desired actions and outcomes (see page 120 for details on the analytic framework). Empowerment is treated as dependent on the interplay of two inter-related factors: agency and opportunity structure. Agency is defined as an actor's ability to make meaningful choices; that is, the actor is able to envisage and purposively choose options. Opportunity structure is defined as those aspects of the context within which actors operate that affect their ability to transform agency into effective action. Central to this is the understanding that imbalances in power relations affect people's capacity to make effective choices and benefit from poverty reduction efforts. For the Bank's Empowerment Team, this approach to empowerment has direct relevance to rights-based approaches to development, which—depending on one's perspective—are based on a sense of justice and equity in relations between people, as well as on the idea that individuals have a set of entitlements that the state is responsible to advance, promote, and protect.

The papers and two-day discussion enhanced participants' understanding of the discourse on power and rights, but the focus of discussion remained practical. Changing power relations and supporting the realization of human rights essentially means promoting social change. This can, at times, be highly sensitive to partner countries' administrations. In addition, depending on the interpretation of the World Bank's articles that stress its economic mission, donor agencies must consider the extent to which empowerment and rights-based approaches may impinge on the political affairs of member countries. The following synopsis of papers and issues demonstrates that empowerment and rights-based approaches can and should remain on the development agenda of the World Bank and DFID, but that the manner in which they are translated into action needs to be carefully tailored to country and organizational contexts.

Key Messages from the Papers

Rosalind Eyben opened the meeting with her paper "Linking Power and Poverty Reduction." Her overarching message is that there are numerous ways in which power can be conceptualized. In order to design effective strategies, development practitioners must be aware of how they conceive power as well as how those with whom they work conceive power. Eyben focuses on the theoretical underpinnings of power and links these to development practice. She emphasizes that our perceptions of power are influenced by our positions and experiences, and that we should not seek a single conceptual understanding of power. Eyben begins by assuming that our interest in power derives from a common concern with pro-poor change and that we are interested in using the lens of power to make our work more effective. She then draws out different aspects and concepts of power that emerge in theoretical discussions. These include:

- *Power to*: power is the capacity to have an effect.
- *Power over*: power is relational and about social action.
- *Power is knowledge*: knowledge is contingent on our time and place and the power relations that shape our lives. Development efforts often fail because they treat knowledge as information, rather than as the construction of meaning.
- *Power with*: power to develop common ground among different interests and build collective strength.
- *Power structures:* power is embedded in the relationships that shape

how one person or organization has more than others of all of the above.

These messages have several implications for the Bank and DFID. First, as representatives of international development agencies, staff and consultants of both organizations need to be keenly aware of the position they occupy relative to client governments and colleagues—both national and international—working within countries. Next, the power to influence agendas through discourse, direct action, or information disclosure varies according to context. However, the way in which that power is used should be tempered with an understanding of how we perceive power relations within a country and how that aligns with or differs from local perceptions and interests in changing power relations. As Eyben notes, particularly for organizations such as the Bank, the interest in power relations stems from a desire to bring about pro-poor change. In certain situations, however, those of us with our roots in a Western democratic tradition may have views on the route to pro-poor change that may not be the most effective in certain settings. For example, the positive association between decentralization—as a logical outcome of democratization—and poverty reduction is not yet proven, but many of us continue to advocate fiscal, administrative, and political decentralization, citing pro-poor growth as our justification.

In the next paper, **Caroline Moser** argues that successful poverty reduction depends on providing opportunities for poor people to contest their rights through normative changes, including through legal frameworks. In addition to having these frameworks in place, poor people must be able to enhance their capacities and mobilize. Drawing on the framework outlined in Moser and Norton (2001), Moser defines rights as legitimate claims that give rise to correlative obligations or duties. Underlying this is the implicit requirement that some structure of power or authority must be able to confer legitimacy on the claim being made. Moser's paper makes the following points:

- The history of human rights is linked with the UN system. Human rights consists of both legal obligations, such as laws and treaties, as well as a broader set of morally binding ethical and political obligations. The key normative principles include: universality and indivisibility; equality and non-discrimination; participation and inclusion; accountability and the rule of law. There are also customary and religious rights validated through micro-level structures.

- Rights-based approaches suggest a switch from a technical to a political understanding of development. Key components of rights-bases approaches include the premises that (1) people have rights, (2) governments have obligations, and (3) people's participation is central.
- The Bank distinguishes between the indirect and direct promotion of rights. Because human rights are not possible without development, the Bank argues, it promotes rights indirectly as economic and social rights are fulfilled through growth.
- By introducing notions of power into project implementation, practitioners can help empowerment become a mainstream component of development work. This requires work on three levels: (1) normative, beginning with the global legitimacy that human rights have acquired; (2) analytical, identifying the social and political processes that empower or disempower people in different arenas of negotiation; and (3) operational, using a rights-based approach to identify entry points for strengthening capacities of poor people.
- Negotiation over rights can be seen as arenas of contestation in which the structures of power and authority are manifest.

For the Bank and DFID, a rights perspective brings power relations center stage in poverty reduction. Without power—enshrined in formal institutions and backed with adequate human capabilities—poor people cannot successfully contest their rights. As Moser makes clear, empowering poor people in this way transforms the historically technical agendas of development agencies into political agendas, even if development organizations do not explicitly recognize this change.

The Bank's emphasis on its indirect promotion of rights underscores where strategic decisions on what is organizationally possible become critical, particularly for the Bank, whose mandate is limited to economic considerations, but also for DFID, which works in partnership with sovereign governments. How far can development agencies go in furthering an agenda that can be perceived as more internationally than internally driven? How far can it be argued that human rights are not only intrinsically beyond valuation but also have an instrumental value in poverty reduction and growth? These remain key questions that each organization will address during internal discussions on where to take its programs that seek to reduce poverty and enhance equity.

In his paper, **David Mosse** expands on these issues, arguing that effectively changing power relations and empowering poor people always involve influencing political structures and processes to change the relative position of the poor. Mosse describes a number of different ways of thinking about power and then reviews different approaches to empowerment. These approaches include:

- Capacity-building efforts, which emphasize *power to*, view power as an infinitely expanding resource. The counter to this is a struggle for resources, seeking *power over*, which is pursued by activist groups and social movements.
- Empowerment efforts from the bottom up, such as community-driven development (CDD), can address real needs and are more inclusive than elite-dominated local governments. However, these interventions may limit poor people's potential to enhance political capabilities by de-mobilizing them.
- Making poverty a public, moral, and political issue often helps the poor gain leverage. Rights-based approaches are similarly dependent on politicization. One problem with bringing empowerment issues into the political sphere is that political capacity is gained at the cost of conceding power to a political system and its own autonomous logic, which may be less than hospitable to poor people.

Mosse places this discussion in the context of rural development programs in India that use CDD-type models. He compares the states of Andhra Pradesh and Madhya Pradesh, and makes two key points: (1) unequal power relations in many cases shape the way CDD programs are executed, and they tend to affirm existing power structures; and (2) program structures and success are influenced by political interests of the government in power and historically formed social structures.

While experts debate the relative costs of the poor conceding power to a political system by engaging with it, the lessons for the Bank and DFID's work using CDD approaches are important. Following on Moser's definition of rights-based approaches in which individuals can exercise rights only against authorities obligated to recognize and protect those rights, Mosse notes that CDD projects, by creating non-state implementing agencies, often do not go very far in empowering people because they "establish authorities against which rights cannot be asserted." Development agencies operating at the scale of the Bank and DFID can tend towards a rather simplistic belief that externally invoked interventions can change power structures in a sustainable manner. The post-project collapse of many organizations responsible for local level collective action and the concomitant reduction of benefit streams testify to the actual fragility of new structures. Mosse indicates a need for more deeply rooted structural change in both pre- and post-project implementation institutions.

Moving these ideas forward, **Jonathan Fox** suggests that pro-poor reform initiatives will have broader and deeper institutional impacts if they are accompanied by interaction between policymakers and civil society. Fox focuses on the relationship between formal and informal power relations in the process of institutional change. He seeks to identify ways to change the balance of power between pro-reform and anti-reform actors, which requires modifications within the state, within society, and at the state-society interface. Tipping the balance involves a process in which reformers within institutions encourage enabling policy environments, and poor people's organizations scale up to gain monitoring capacity and bargaining power to offset anti-poor elements within institutions.

Fox identifies four key operational issues:

- Rights and empowerment approaches can be mutually supportive in practice, but they remain analytically distinct;
- Empowering reforms are more likely in institutions where pro-reform power is stronger than anti-reform voices;
- The power of pro- or anti-reform actors is based on economies of scale, which improve bargaining power and enable better information through sharing across locations and sectors;
- Participatory governance, or state-society power-sharing over public sector management and resource allocation, can be successful in creating win-win solutions for communities (improved services) and governments (less costly services). However, where the informal

distribution of power is highly imbalanced, local elites can capture these processes.

Fox uses four examples of rural development programs in Mexico to show that programs are most successful where social organizations have the capacity and willingness to participate, and where factions within formal implementing agencies (both at the top and middle levels) are willing to take risks in partnering with social organizations.

Fox points to the need to monitor development interventions closely to ensure that elites do not capture the outcomes. He also states that DFID and the Bank should expect higher returns in countries where pro-reform voices are already strong. In these countries, well placed investments would include focusing on enactment and enforcement of pro-poor legislation, disseminating information, and enabling pro-reform campaigners to increase their support. However, reflecting Moser's earlier comments, Fox also stresses that nominal rights granted by institutions are insufficient for empowerment without capacities among the disempowered to exercise those rights. It is not enough to seek institutional change alone; citizens also have to be equipped with the capabilities to utilize opportunities.

Jeremy Holland and **Simon Brook** continue the focus on development practice. Holland and Brook state that measuring empowerment at the national level requires an extensive effort to combine data from a variety of sources (mostly household surveys) with qualitative probing of institutional processes and new survey modules to generate information on different empowerment outcomes. Holland and Brook focus on developing a set of indicators for measuring empowerment at the national level. They emphasize that measuring empowerment is hindered by three factors: the lack of a universal definition; the intangible and non-material nature of empowerment as bound up in institutions and processes; and the contextual nature of those institutions and processes. They insist that a universal—or at least broadly relevant—definition of empowerment and a set of observable, objective, and measurable indicators are necessary to measure progress toward empowerment. Holland and Brook suggest three types of indicators: (1) data generated through household and other surveys; (2) intermediate and direct indicators derived from existing survey instruments; and (3) indicators not yet captured by existing instruments. Using the analytic framework designed by the World Bank Empowerment Team (see page 120),

Holland and Brook note that measures of individual agency are already generated by several existing instruments, such as the Living Standards Measurement Survey. Measuring opportunity structure, however, is not easily captured by household survey instruments. In this case, researchers must use a mixed-method approach that includes tracking legislation, regulation, and procedure at the national level, and probing the operation of formal and informal institutions at the local level. Finally, Holland and Brook highlight potential direct indicators of empowerment related to four forms of empowerment (passive access, active participation, influence, and control), noting that these are not yet available and will need to be gathered through a new module currently under construction.

Whereas Eyben emphasizes that we should not seek common definitions and conceptual understandings, and Mosse concurs that empowerment "requires a broad framework," Holland and Brook argue that the lack of a common definition of empowerment is a central difficulty in measuring it. For development agencies such as DFID and the Bank, who have numerous staff and work with a large number of partners, having a clear definition and framework is pragmatic. However, the warnings need heeding. As experience and evidence accrue, it is simply good practice to review and re-examine these constructs as a matter of course. Clearly, however, Holland and Brook's paper demonstrates that much more work is required now if we are to know what our achievements are in relation to empowerment. The Bank has a workable definition of empowerment, but it recognizes that currently there is a dearth of robust and reliable analysis that allows development agencies, governments, and citizens to understand what progress is being made in relation to enhancing the position of poor and marginalized people. Similarly, there is a surprising lack of analysis documenting the association between empowerment and poverty. Therefore, not only do agencies need to be better equipped with indicators and instruments for tracking empowerment at the national and intervention level, there is also an immediate need to generate research exploring the association between power relations and poverty.

In the final paper, "Empowerment at the Local Level," **Michael Woolcock** states that if we are to pursue empowerment, we need to get serious about it by showing that exclusion is a problem, designing approachable and viable programs to promote empowerment, and monitoring those programs in ways that clearly show their benefits. According to Woolcock, to understand why certain groups persistently achieve poor development outcomes, we must:

- identify more clearly who is excluded, why it matters, and how this exclusion is created and sustained. This requires bringing a greater conceptual and empirical rigor to debates around empowerment and exclusion. This research will always be controversial because data do not fit easily with the usual imperatives of large organizations. The way forward is a two-fold commitment to (1) expanding and improving existing household sources on development outcomes and their determinants, and (2) engaging in more context- and issues-specific research using mixed methods to understand the processes.
- identify appropriate policy responses that are technically sound, politically supportable, and administratively implementable. Those promoting empowerment often do so in excessively abstract terms, which are easy to dismiss or ignore. These abstractions must be replaced by viable, usable responses to exclusion and disempowerment. If they don't meet these criteria, they often become part of the problem.
- demonstrate the efficacy of our responses. We must show more precisely the value added of empowerment-specific responses, where it lies, and how it can be improved. This means putting considerable resources into carefully designing an evaluation strategy that disentangles project impacts from non-project impacts to show the value of an empowerment approach compared with the alternatives.

There is a parallel between a normative/analytical/operational framework suggested by Moser (and Norton) for introducing a rights-based approach, and Woolcock's technically sound/politically supportable/administratively implementable approach. These authors emphasize that care must be taken to pursue approaches that will show results, rather than to confuse the issue and overgeneralize the importance of empowering approaches. Woolcock also indicates that if the Bank and DFID are going to advocate empowerment, then these organizations need to do it better. The practical options offered reflect the concerns of many of the meeting's participants. We need good research and improved measurement tools. We need to work on both the operational and policy side of the issue. And finally, we need to articulate what is meant by empowerment.

Cross-cutting Issues

A common theme in the workshop papers and discussions is the many different ways in which power can be conceptualized, understood, and translated into action. Development agencies, including DFID and the Bank, have very diverse understandings of empowerment and rights. Given that these agencies are powerful actors in their own right, papers and discussions repeatedly emphasize the need to generate conceptual clarity. A de-politicized view of empowerment (based on the *power to* formulation) can lead to donor agencies engaging in capacity-building activities that may reinforce power relations that are unfavorable to many poor people. As Fox and Mosse observe, elites are likely to capture the benefits of community development activities in environments where informal power relations are highly unequal.

This observation implies that donor agencies must understand their own position and the implications of their own actions. Two directions for institutional change follow. First, as part of their process of developing strategies, development actors need to ask questions about the likely impact of their actions on power relationships in the short and long term. All development activities—from building a road to providing budget support directly to governments—influence the evolution of power relations. Whether practitioners do this in ways that will strengthen the position of poor people or erode it is a key question, but one that is rarely factored into a decision-making process that remains largely technocratic in character.

Second, to develop implementable and realistic policy options, donor agencies must understand the political context of the environments they work in (whether national, international, or local). There is a persistent sense that the emergence of poverty as an issue in formal political arenas—and of categories of the poor as politicians' constituencies—is a key feature of situations where rapid pro-poor change is likely to happen. Development agencies have little control over emerging political projects that create incentives for political participation among hitherto excluded populations. But it is helpful to have the capacity to analyze such processes and recognize where the potential for transformational change may be located.

Unsurprisingly, participants emphasized the importance of strengthening poor people's capability to make effective challenges to the prevailing pattern of power relationships. Moser emphasizes the capacity to mobilize to make claims, and she contrasts the success of broad-based mobilization strategies adopted by squatter associations in a number of countries with the difficulties that slum dwellers in Guayaquil, Ecuador, have had in asserting their theoretical rights to land. In practice, most slum dwellers are incapable of negotiating the legal labyrinth involved in acquiring title to their land. In contrast, there has been a proliferating success of bottom-up mobilizations of urban poor associations in a range of countries including Zimbabwe, South Africa, Thailand, and the Philippines. Eyben describes DFID's efforts to persuade the Government of Bolivia to include (as part of its PRSP theme on exclusion) strategies for issuing identity cards to those who lack them. Possessing identity cards considerably increases poor people's potential to successfully assert rights in a number of arenas. But the engagement of donor agencies can undermine as easily as reinforce the capacity of poor people to make claims and challenge patterns of power relations that lead to their exploitation or exclusion. To make a productive contribution, development agencies need an informed understanding of the realities of social and political change.

Ultimately, empowerment and rights approaches to development are coterminous, though the strategies that development organizations such as DFID and the Bank deploy to achieve these final ends may differ. While decisions on short-term objectives and particular activities may be specific to each organization, a clear message emerged from the meeting that development agencies must not only work to enhance the capabilities of disempowered and disenfranchised citizens, but also must ensure that the enabling environment is conducive to equalizing opportunity for all.

References

Moser, Caroline, and Andy Norton. 2001. *To claim our rights: Livelihood security, human rights and sustainable development.* London: Overseas Development Institute.

2. Linking Power and Poverty Reduction

Rosalind Eyben, Institute of Development Studies

How any one of us thinks and feels about power depends on a number of factors:

- the identities ascribed to us in childhood, such as female, black, middle class, Moslem, American ... and the identities that we choose for ourselves, such as feminist, internationalist, anti-racist, hedonist, Buddhist;
- the way of thinking about how the world works that we learned from how we have been educated and the disciplines we have specialized in, for example, sociology, economics, engineering;
- the trajectory of our engagement with development; our career and current professional locus;
- other contingent life events that have shaped our intellectual and emotional understanding of why the world is as it is; how we fit into that world, and how we would like that world to change or to stay as it is.

All of these factors come into play in any exchange of views on the themes of power, empowerment, and poverty reduction. They also provide the backdrop to this selective review of concepts in a highly complex and contested field of study.

Whatever our differences in views and understandings, I assume that our interest in power derives from a shared concern with pro-poor change. By pro-poor change, I understand a change in the political, economic, and social structures and systems of a country that will facilitate the achievement of the Millennium Development Goals. Note, however that structures and systems are themselves conceptual statements that are subject to debate. I will return to this issue later.

I also assume that we are interested in the practical implications of our analysis. How can the lens of power enable development organizations like the World Bank and DFID to be more effective in supporting pro-poor change? This means factoring into the analysis ourselves, and the organizations that we represent, as potentially powerful agents in the development arena. By potentially powerful, I mean that we have the capacity to effect positive change, but the extent to which we realize that capacity depends on how we work with other organizations and actors. If we work without any clear and explicit conceptual underpinning, we may find that we are perpetuating those very systems that we strive to change.[1]

I do not take the position that the international aid system is part of a global power structure that necessarily reproduces rather than reduces poverty. We have many examples of aid contributing to greater social justice and equity. There are also examples of aid making things worse. Greater conceptual clarity can help us do more good and less harm.

In this paper, I look at some definitions and concepts of power. Rather than strive to agree on a single concept that can explain every circumstance, I propose we accept that different concepts may be more or less helpful in illuminating particular development challenges in specific local contexts.

Conceiving Power

Power has been understood in many different ways. What follows is a very selective discussion of approaches that can be useful for development practice.[2]

---

1. Conceptual underpinnings are what Midgley (1996) calls "philosophical plumbing" and Giddens (1984) calls "discursive consciousness."

2. Haugaard (2002,1) provides a very helpful schematic diagram showing the historical evolution of different concepts of power in the Western intellectual tradition.

Power To

On the World Bank's Web site, there are over 900 entries for reports on the subject of "power." Yes, they are about electricity and other energy projects! Nevertheless, it is a good starting point for a broad definition. Power is the energy that causes change—or prevents change from happening. According to one dictionary, "Power is the capacity to have an effect." We can describe this as *power to*.

This understanding of power informs the capability approach of Amartya Sen (1995), who asserts that people are not free when they do not have the power to make choices about their lives. Sen concludes that utilitarian preference theory cannot be the basis for justice because very deprived people, for example, many women, tend to limit their preferences, thereby constraining their freedom. Sen sees relations between men and women in terms of "co-operative conflicts" in which men have a capability advantage. While some social scientists argue that these current arrangements create optimal socioeconomic efficiency, Sen insists upon the need to identify alternative co-operative conflicts that are no less efficient and more equitable.

The interplay of the lack of different aspects of *power to* within the household and within the wider economy are well described in a study of farm laborers in the fruit growing area of South Africa and summarized in box 1 below.

Power to is about agency.[3] It relates to the way the World Bank has used the term *empowerment*, as set out in its *World Development Report 2000/2001* (2000), and then further elaborated in Deepa Narayan's *Empowerment and Poverty Reduction Sourcebook* (2002). Narayan notes that powerlessness—that is, not being able to choose and act as one would wish—can occur on several levels, in households as well as in institutions. Narayan focuses on institutions because that is where she sees the crux of the Bank's work for poverty reduction. Hence, she defines empowerment as "the expansion of assets and capabilities of poor people to participate in, negotiate with, influence, control and hold accountable institutions that affect their lives" (Narayan 2002, xviii). Her argument concentrates more on action by the poor (rather than by the state) to improve their own lives at the local level.[4]

---

3. Agency is about intention or consciousness of action, sometimes with the implication of choices between alternative actions.

4. For a recent review of the various criticisms of the World Bank's earlier positions on empowerment, see Kwok-Fu Wong (2003).

Box 1. Poverty and Agency in South Africa

In a study of farm laborers in the citrus-producing area of South Africa, du Toit argues that any attempt to understand chronic poverty needs to begin and end with the issue of the intimate and mutually reinforcing links between income poverty and a poor household's lack of social power. Women laborers' lack of the basic assets necessary for household food production or entrepreneurial activity—and their consequent dependence on insecure paid jobs and on networks of patronage—renders them profoundly marginal in the society to which they have been adversely incorporated. The author's policy recommendations include a reformed welfare system and other government interventions, as well as support to "empowerment" of local communities, bearing in mind the challenge of working against the disempowering effects of patriarchal gender relations.

Source: Andries du Toit, 2003.

The World Bank's current understanding of empowerment, as set out in a note by Alsop, Heinsohn, and Somma (2004) was developed to address some of the criticisms of Narayan's approach. This understanding includes the idea of effective choice, and introduces structure (institutional formal and informal rules of the game) as a central issue and as a constraint to agency. Empowerment is also understood as being more than agency at the local level, allowing for possible action at intermediary and macro (national) levels.

Both of these Bank approaches to empowerment derive from a liberal position that values autonomy as an attribute of individuals rather than participation as a social achievement for the general good of the polity. From that perspective, participation is understood as an instrument for enhanced efficiency: it tackles the problem of the self-interested public official and it can help services fit more closely with what people want. This view of empowerment can be critiqued because of an underlying assumption that public servants are typically self-serving, rather than altruistic (Le Grand 2003).

It is worth noting that any government's policy approaches to empowerment and participation may well reflect not only the currently popular liberal approach but also other conceptual traditions that contradict or challenge such an approach. Policymakers are often muddled or pragmatic, responding to different pressures and points of view, rarely inspecting the philosophical plumbing that drives their decisions, as illustrated in box 2 below, which draws on my own observations and those of Needham (2003).

VeneKlasen and Miller (2002) present a more explicitly political understanding of empowerment. They provide frameworks that build on ideas of collective consciousness-building leading to strong and balanced citizen-state relations. Mick Moore (2001) argues that donors might do better to turn their attention to helping to create the political conditions in which poor people can organize politically, rather than seeking to support social service organizations for the poor. Moore suggests that, for international development agencies, this requires a subtle and nuanced understanding of politics and political action. He implies that such an approach may well be beyond their capacity. After his paper was published, DFID, through the work of Sue Unsworth (2003), has directed more attention to the need for good political analysis, but it remains an issue as to whether development bureaucracies can make good use of such analysis.

These alternative views on empowerment lead us to other ways of thinking about power that I shall now discuss.

Power Over

Returning to the dictionary, we find that power is not only the ability to do something, but also to act upon a person or thing. Power becomes relational. It is about social action. Robinson Crusoe in isolation had the power to chop

---

BOX 2. POVERTY AND EMPOWERMENT IN THE UK

The UK government's strategy for poverty reduction in deprived areas of England and Wales has a three-fold approach to community participation that reflects different conceptual perspectives. Participation is seen as having a role in building and maintaining social capital (cohesion), in making services more effective and efficient, and in addressing the perceived problem of the democratic deficit. Enhanced citizen participation is thus understood not just as a means to more effective service delivery but as important in its own right because of its potential for personal empowerment and active citizenship. Different philosophical perspectives within the government (neo-liberalism, communitarianism, civic republicanism) result in some confusion as to the meaning of empowerment and citizenship and thus their implications for policy priorities and practice.

down a tree. Relational power came into play when Man Friday arrived on the island.

In international aid, euphemisms are often used for power over. For example, the World Bank's Country Assistance Strategy for India (2001) speaks of "the constraints that inhibit and exclude people from participating in and sharing the benefits of development." What would be the impact on the Bank's relations with the Government of India if this were to be re-worded to read "the exercise of power that inhibits and excludes people from participating in and sharing the benefits of development"? Another common euphemism is "entrenched hierarchy." We may wish to reflect on why it is so difficult to discuss easily the issue of some people having structural, political, economic, and social power over others.

> "WE MAY WISH TO REFLECT ON WHY IT IS SO DIFFICULT TO DISCUSS EASILY THE ISSUE OF SOME PEOPLE HAVING STRUCTURAL, POLITICAL, ECONOMIC, AND SOCIAL POWER OVER OTHERS."

Thinking about power as *power over* others has long-standing roots in the social sciences and in political theory. Much of the debate on this topic in the last century was about whether power should be conceived solely in relation to public decision making or in a wider sense as diffused in other relationships such as economic or domestic ones. Stephen Lukes' theory of the three dimensions of power (1974) looks at the institutional and cultural structures that enable A to have power over B. John Gaventa (1980) used this theory to explain what he found in the Appalachians, where less powerful community members did not challenge visible power in ostensibly open fora, such as public meetings. This was in part due to a history of force and discretionary resource distribution that maintained hidden power, but it was also due to invisible power—an internalization of community members' sense of powerlessness. These three faces of power prevented them from challenging their state of impoverishment.

Invisible power is rooted in the Marxist idea of "false consciousness." It has been a popular concept in feminism and other social movements that seek to liberate people through knowledge of how the world objectively works. "Knowledge is power in the hands of the workers" reads the inscription above the front door to a trade union education center in Yorkshire.

Associated with *power over* is the idea of hegemony, understanding the way the world is as being the only way the world could be. We can recognize the existence of hegemony when we understand a certain social, economic, or political practice as "natural." Such an understanding cannot be challenged because we cannot imagine other possibilities. Unlike a hegemonic belief, an ideological belief can be challenged. It is helpful to think of a continuum from hegemony to ideology. Whereas hegemony means that we cannot imagine alternatives, ideology is just one view among other possibilities of how the world should be. Thus, at a particular moment in time and place there may be present more than one "truth."[5] Of course, one ideology may be more hegemonic and harder to resist than an alternative, but we could imagine a stronger capacity to challenge *power over* as we move along that continuum from hegemony to a condition in which all ideologies have equal status. We can then inquire as to whether one way of understanding social change is to see it as a process by which hegemony is resisted and transformed into something that can be rejected. An example is the practice of untouchability in India, where what was thought to be "natural" is now changing to reveal prejudice and discrimination in its place.

Not all resistance openly challenges hegemony, but seeks to make life slightly less uncomfortable within the existing power regime. Scott (1985) has suggested that the relationship between dominant elites and subordinates is a struggle in which both sides are continually probing for weakness and exploiting small advantages—"the weapons of the weak."

People may also resist the exercise of power but not the premises that make that exercise possible. This is the difference between getting rid of a bad king and deciding that kingship itself is bad. Resistance is an adaptive mechanism that may take advantage of (and thus unintentionally reproduce) the very rules of the game that keeps the resister subordinate (by replacing a bad king with a good king). However, Gledhill (2000) notes the importance of analyzing the content of such popular practices of resistance in order to see what kind of impact they have on power relations. We should not see such resistance as an either/or situation, as letting off steam (which re-establishes stability and equilibrium), or as an expression of real revolution.

---

5. I am using "ideology" in the meaning of a truth-thought system, not in the meaning of standing in opposition to something else which is supposed to count as "objective" truth (see Foucault 1980, 118-119).

Power With and Power Within

Concepts of *power with* and *power within* originated in feminism and other social movements. Many people in a subordinate position may question the way the world is ordered but do not organize for strategic resistance because they fear the consequences should they fail. They would need to gain support from others to develop new ways of understanding—or frameworks of meaning—about how the world could work. What are the conditions that allow for the mobilization of such support? *Power with* is a term that describes common ground among different interests and the building of collective strength through organization and the development of shared values and strategies. DFID's and the World Bank's interest in moving beyond their traditional support to service delivery NGOs may lead to an engagement with social movements and community and interest-based organizations that have developed a voice and a capacity to influence change through the strength of *power with*. While *power with* is often thought of as collective action in response to powerlessness, it is an equally useful concept in considering powerfulness, as for example with Adam Smith's cartel of a butcher, baker, and candlestick–maker—or indeed of development agencies.

Power to organize is related to a person's self-worth and sense of dignity that has been described as *power within*. There has been a long-standing tradition of civil society activity, such as Action Aid's REFLECT, based on Freirian principles that seek to enhance the power within.

Power Everywhere

The broadest view of power focuses on the everyday practices of all aspects of social life. We are shifting from an idea of *power over* to one of *power everywhere*. This provides a view in which every one of us is implicated in the performance of power, each time we walk into a room or participate in a workshop. Feminism and Foucault come together in the idea that power exists not only at the institutional level but also in our daily lives. The personal becomes the political.

Power/Knowledge

Postmodern theory has challenged the idea of objective value-free knowledge, de-linked from power. Knowledge—how we understand and describe the world—is contingent on our time and place and the relations of power that shape our lives. For Foucault, power and knowledge are inseparable. Power/ knowledge works through discourses that frame what is thinkable and doable. Discourses are not only the way that things are said or written, but also concrete activities associated with words, such as Log Frames or PRSPs in a development setting. Through deconstruction of discourses, closely examining the concepts, practices, statements, and beliefs associated with them, Foucault showed that the effects of power could be made visible. Thus, the first step to changing power relations is to deconstruct a discourse to reveal it for what it is.

Foucault's interest in what we know and how we know it is important for development practice. His discussion (1980) of historical amnesia—what is forgotten by those with the power to construct knowledge—is particularly relevant. Critics of "development" argue that we collectively suffer from this amnesia. Their critique raises important questions in a debate on the problem of the politics of knowledge. What are the power implications of the fact that most research in developing countries is being funded by international development organizations such as the World Bank or DFID? Does it matter who owns the knowledge if we think this is the means to achieving the Millennium Development Goals? Alternatively, does our understanding of "development" and the power of our knowledge constrain their achievement?

Power Structures

We often think of power as a thing that we possess in greater or lesser amounts. But we can also think about the relationships that shape how a person or organization acquires more *power to*, *power with*, *power within*, and *power over*. When power relations repeat themselves and form a pattern, they become institutionalized; they become the rules of the game.

In his work on frameworks of power, Clegg (1989) proposes three interlocking levels, or circuits, of power. The most visible is "episodic agency" in which one agent exercises power over another, for example, when a police officer imposes a traffic fine on a speeding motorist. This event of one agent exercising power over another is defined and shaped by the rules, relations, and resources (structure or dispositional arrangements) that constitute the episodic power that is visible in the relation between police officer and traffic offender. These structures are in turn shaped by the more fundamental systemic forces that define the rules of the game. Each time A gets B to do what A wants, A is not only achieving a desired outcome but is also confirming the dispositional arrangements of the game and reinforcing and maintaining the overall system.   Using a chess analogy, Clegg invites us to think about the dispositional arrangements that give queens more moves than pawns, and to consider the extent to which deeper systemic properties may allow the most powerful piece on the board, the queen, to reinterpret the rules so she can move not only as a queen but also as a knight.   What chance does a pawn have in such circumstances?   How can individual agency affect these fundamental systemic forces in which the rules of the game are established to benefit the powerful?

Despite everything however, Clegg argues, changes in power relations can and do take place. They occur by collective agency, such as social movements, "outflanking" dispositional arrangements through networks and alliances that take advantage of points of instability.

Structures of Power in Bolivia

Clegg's framework illuminates a process of change in which I was involved when working for DFID in Bolivia: In 2001, the Bolivian government found it unacceptable for donors to discuss a particular issue in policy dialogue; but over the space of three years, the issue became an accepted government and donor priority. The matter concerned DFID and Sida support of efforts by a section of Bolivian civil society to heighten awareness about undocumented citizens. A significant number of indigenous people in Bolivia are without identity documents, excluding them in a variety of ways from economic, social, and political life, and contributing to livelihood insecurity and lack of voice (León et al. 2003).   Previously, development agencies had responded technically to this problem by providing the authorities with new computer systems; thus, they had intervened at the "episodic" level without analyzing the dispositional arrangements that continued to prevent people from acquiring identity cards because of the way the bureaucracy functioned.   As the issue gained more prominence, some of those affected asked DFID and Sida to provide the funds to pay lawyers to process individual cases of undocumented individuals. If we had agreed to this, such support, once again at the episodic level, would have reinforced rather than changed the existing circuits of power.   I wrote at the time in a field visit report:

> Even if the organisations in the Consortium were able to assist directly everyone in those communities where they are currently working, this would still leave all the people in the rest of Bolivia without help. I discussed with

them how the strategic vision of the Consortium should not be neglected in their understandable anxiety to help particular communities. The current incredibly Byzantine identity card system appears to be designed (consciously or unconsciously) by the State to deny full citizenship rights to a very large number of people in Bolivia.

A participant at one meeting I attended proposed a radical solution that mocked and challenged the system itself—the third circuit of power. One way—in theory if not in bureaucratic practice—to obtain an identity card was to show a baptism certificate. His idea was a mass-baptism of undocumented citizens performed by a sympathetic priest in a public ceremony and then a march on the capital city, La Paz, with the newly baptized holding their certificates and demanding justice. Thus, the focus of effort shifted from seeking redress for individual problems within the existing dispositional arrangements to considering collective action for changing those arrangements and possibly threatening the deeper historically derived structures of power in Bolivia. Donor support helped create the conditions for bringing this issue to the national consciousness and making it a subject of priority for the incoming administration in October 2003.

In this matter, I was engaged in a complex web of power relations in which my personal agency and analytical capacity were both supported and challenged by macro-level dispositional and structural powers. My position as a donor in an aid-dependent country gave me the authority to analyze social situations in the country and the power to help make visible to national policymakers an injustice that they had tacitly chosen to disregard. At the same time, influential people in and outside government actively discouraged me from becoming involved, accusing me of starting a "donor-driven" initiative and of not understanding the real situation. They objected to the power of the donor to analyze a situation and provide the means to tackle a problem they did not see as a priority. On the other hand, I interpreted their objections as a reflection of their (unstated) concern that tackling the identity card issue might contribute to an empowerment process threatening the existing power structures (Eyben and León, forthcoming).

Conclusion: Reflexive Engagement With Unpredictability

I began this paper with the comment that how any one of us thinks and feels about power depends on a number of factors, and in the story I just told, my analysis and actions were shaped both by my position in the aid system and by my personal history. I conclude by briefly returning to this reflexive theme and relating it to the challenge of unpredictability.

Development agencies are political actors. They use their power/knowledge to define a problem, getting others to agree with them by constructing alliances and networks to sustain the analysis. Our analysis itself is thus part of the process of exercising power. As the way we tend to problematize is specifically along the rational lines of cause and effect, we assume that certain actions will lead to certain other effects, seeking to control the process by defining the parameters for action. In the case of the Bolivian identity cards, I could not have predicted the results of the donor support as one contributing factor to a complex process of political change taking place in the country during the last three years. Was our support more useful because we could not predict the outcome?

Michel de Certeau (1988) argues that the use of tactics is less about being able to have a clear idea of the future and the power to achieve one's desired goals than it is about the small acts through which people without power can claw back some control and recuperate some sense of their own agency, in situations that are contingent, constantly changing, forever uncertain.[6] This resonates with contemporary thinking about the need for public policy to take a complex adaptive system, rather than a command and control approach (Chapman 2002, Eyben 2004).

As development actors, we can recognize the fiction of being in control when we include ourselves in the analysis. We are actors in the play rather than the person directing it. This means asking questions about who we are and why we understand the world in a certain way because of who we are. How does that understanding affect what our organizations do and the way we relate to others? What criteria do we use in deciding with whom we work and whom to support? What knowledge informs those criteria? These questions require us to reflect on our own power and the dilemmas of engagement in other people's struggles, such as the one I described in Bolivia. How should we use our power? When should we be tentative, rather than certain, and modest rather than ambitious? Can good, grounded, conceptual power analysis guide us as to when we should or should not become involved? Is this a practice that development agencies can aspire to?

---

6. I am grateful to Andrea Cornwall for drawing this thinking by de Certeau to my attention and for her commenting overall on the first draft of this paper.

References

Alsop, Ruth, N. Heinsohn, and A. Somma. 2004. *Measuring empowerment: An analytic framework*. Washington, DC: World Bank.

Chapman, Jake. 2002. *System failure: Why governments must learn to think differently*. London: Demos.

Clegg, Stewart. 1989. *Frameworks of power*. London: Sage Publications.

de Certeau, Michel. 1988. *The practice of everyday life*. Trans. Steven F. Rendall. Berkeley: University of California Press.

du Toit, Andries. 2003. Hunger in the valley of fruitfulness: Globalization, "social exclusion" and chronic poverty in Ceres, South Africa. Paper presented at the conference Staying Poor: Chronic Poverty and Development Policy, IDPM, University of Manchester, England. Paper available at http://idpm.man.ac.uk/cprc/ Conference/conferencepapers.htm.

Eyben, Rosalind. 2004. Relationships matter for supporting change in favor of poor people. *Lessons for Change* 6. Brighton: Institute of Development Studies.

Eyben, Rosalind, and Rosario León. Forthcoming. Who owns the gift? Donor-recipient relations and the national elections in Bolivia. In *Anthropology Upstream*. Eds. D. Lewis and D. Mosse. London: Pluto Press.

Foucault, Michel. 1980. *Power/knowledge: Selected interviews and other writings, 1972–1977*. Ed. Colin Gordon. New York: Pantheon.

Gaventa, John. 1980. *Power and powerlessness: Quiescence and rebellion in an Appalachian valley*. Urbana and Chicago: University of Illinois Press.

Giddens, Anthony. 1984. *The constitution of society: Outline of the theory of structuration*. Cambridge, UK: Polity Press.

Gledhill, John. 1994 (2000). *Power and its disguises: Anthropological perspectives on politics*. London: Pluto.

Haugaard, Mark. 2002. *Power: A reader*. Manchester: Manchester University Press.

Le Grand, Julian. 2003. *Motivation, agency and public policy: Of knights and knaves, pawns and queens*. Oxford, UK: Oxford University Press.

León, Rosario, Jay Goulden, Carmen Rea, Huberto Salinas, Luis Medrano, and Jan Schollaert. 2003. Social exclusion, rights and chronic poverty in Bolivia. Paper presented at the conference Staying Poor: Chronic Poverty and Development Policy, IDPM, University of Manchester, England. Paper available at http://idpm.man.ac.uk/cprc/Conference/conferencepapers.htm.

Lukes, Steven. 1974. *Power: A radical view*. London: Macmillan.

Midgley, Mary. 1996. *Utopias, dolphins and computers*. London: Routledge.

Moore, Mick. 2001. Empowerment at last? *Journal of International Development* 13: 321–9.

Narayan, Deepa, ed. 2002. *Empowerment and poverty reduction: A sourcebook.* Washington, DC: World Bank.

Needham, Catherine. 2003. Citizen-consumers: New labour's marketplace democracy. A Catalyst Working Paper. The Catalyst Forum. http://www.catalystforum.org.uk/pubs/index.html.

Scott, James C. 1985. *Weapons of the weak: Everyday forms of peasant resistance.* London: Yale University Press.

Sen, Amartya. 1995. Gender inequality and theories of justice. In *Women, Culture, and Development: A Study of Human Capabilities.* Eds. Martha Nussbaum and Jonathan Glover. Oxford: Clarendon Press.

Unsworth, Sue. 2003. Better government for poverty reduction: More effective partnerships for change. Draft Consultation Document, London: DFID.

VeneKlasen, Lisa, with Valerie Miller. 2002. *A new weave of power, people & politics: The action guide for advocacy and citizen participation.* Oklahoma City: World Neighbors.

Wong, Kwok-Fu. 2003. Empowerment as a panacea for poverty—Old wine in new bottles? Reflections on the world bank's conception of power. *Progress in Development Studies* 3 (4): 307–322.

World Bank. 2000. *World development report 2000/2001: Attacking poverty.* New York: Oxford University Press.

———. 2001. *Country assistance strategy for India.* New Delhi: World Bank.

3. Rights, Power, and Poverty Reduction

Caroline Moser, Overseas Development Institute

If the primary emphasis of development policy for the past thirty years has been economic in nature, with the new millennium has come a fundamental shift in focus: the political dimension of development is increasingly identified as the predominant concern in and of itself, and in relation to poverty reduction. Since politics are essentially about power relations, the links between power and poverty are finally on the agenda of international development institutions.

This paper draws heavily on the Overseas Development Institute Working Paper *To Claim Our Rights* (Moser and Norton 2001), commissioned by Steen Jorgenson in the World Bank's Social Development Department as a background paper for the recently completed Social Development Strategy Paper.[1] This paper, also for a World Bank meeting, is written with an awareness of the World Bank's conundrum regarding the relevance of human rights approaches. It is important to be aware of the limitations of providing seemingly technocratic explanations of the comparative advantages or disadvantages of a particular development approach in what some may argue is essentially a political debate.

---

1. However, the final Social Development Strategy (World Bank 2004b) makes no reference to human rights. My sincere thanks to Andy Norton for allowing me to quote liberally from this jointly authored paper. I would like to acknowledge Ruth Alsop's important guidance and support in writing this paper, and I thank Laure-Helene Piron for comments on the first draft.

Introduction to Rights-Based Approaches to Development

This section summarizes a number of basic issues such as definitions, history of rights-based approaches, and central guiding principles.

Definition of Human Rights

Rights are widely characterized as legitimate claims that give rise to correlative obligations or duties. To have a right is to have a legitimate claim against some person, group, or organization, such as a social or economic institution, a state, or an international community. The latter, in turn, has an obligation or a duty to assist the rights holder in securing the right. This is represented in the formula: A has a right against B in relation to C, where A is the rights bearer, B is the duty bearer, and C is the object or end of the right.

This formulation requires the presence of a power or authority that is able to confer legitimacy on the claim being made. Indeed, the definition, interpretation, and implementation of rights are dynamic processes that are inherently political in nature. As such, in relation to development processes, human rights are *a priori* about power relations. In categorizing rights, it may be useful to make a further distinction between rights as legitimate claims; a system of rights, also called a "rights regime"; individual rights; and universal human rights (see box 1).

Summary Issues in the History of Human Rights

The United Nations system is probably the most important rights regime. The UN promotes and protects human rights through international legal, ethical, and political obligations. International legal obligations are a subset of international obligations that pertain to formal international law; namely, international treaties, international custom, the general principles of international law, as well as judicial decisions. International ethical and political obligation are a broader set of morally binding international obligations derived from ethical and political statements, declarations, and commitments made at the UN level.

In the complex history of human rights within the United Nations system, it is useful to clarify the following:

First, the UN's legal competence in human rights lies in the UN Charter, an international treaty that is legally binding on all state members, who are required to comply with its provisions in good faith. Among the principles and purposes of the Charter is the reaffirmation of faith in fundamental human rights, and the promotion and encouragement of respect for human rights and for fundamental freedoms for all people, regardless of race, sex, language, or religion.

Second, the Universal Declaration of Human Rights, adopted as a resolution of the UN General Assembly in 1948, clarified the scope and contents of human rights in the UN Charter. Its 26 articles lay out details of its basic charter principles of equality and non-discrimination (articles 1-2), civil and political rights (articles 3–21), and economic, social, and cultural rights (articles 22–26).

Next, while the Universal Declaration possessed significant moral and political value, it did *not* establish legally binding international obligations upon states. The negotiation process for codifying these human rights into legally binding international treaties began in 1948. A protracted debate ensued before the International Bill on Human Rights comprising the International Covenant on Civil and Political Rights (1966) and the International Covenant on Economic, Social and Cultural Rights (1966) were both finally passed in 1976. Other key international treaties in the field of human rights then followed.

BOX 1. CONCEPTUALIZATIONS OF RIGHTS

Rights as legitimate claims: Rights are widely characterized as legitimate claims that invoke correlative obligations or duties.

Rights regime: A system of rights deriving from a particular regulatory order or source of authority. In a given society, several rights regimes may co-exist (for example, customary law, religious law, and statutory law), each with distinct normative frameworks and means of formulation and enforcement.

Individual rights: A subset of rights as legitimate claims in which the rights bearer is an individual person; group rights would not fall within this subset of rights.

Universal human rights: An individual right with a universal domain; that is, an individual right that applies to all human beings equally, irrespective of their membership of particular families, groups, religions, communities, or societies.

Source: Vizard 2001, Norton 2001.

Finally, in addition to these international legal obligations are the provisions adopted by large numbers of governments at international conferences. These represent important ethical and political commitments and have contributed to setting the standards for human rights in recent years. They include the principle that "all human rights are universal, indivisible, and interdependent and interrelated" adopted at the 1993 Vienna World Conference on Human Rights.[2] The output of international conferences has been extremely important in converting the aspirations of some of the human rights conventions into strategic agendas that can be pursued by development agencies and governments.

Key Principles in Human Rights

As agreed in Vienna in 1993, key normative principles of human rights include the following:

- Universality and indivisibility
- Equality and non-discrimination
- Participation and inclusion
- Accountability and the rule of law

Key normative principles are essential, and different organizations and institutions frequently adopt and adapt those agreed to in the UN conferences. Box 2 provides a synthesis of key normative principles that underlie a human rights approach to development suitable for any organization concerned with poverty reduction and sustainable development.

Since human rights are normative in nature, they have designated rights holders and duty bearers. As primary duty bearers (but by no means the only duty bearers), states have an obligation to protect, promote, and ensure the realization of all human rights. This obligation requires them to ratify human rights treaties and to translate their contents into domestic legislation for rights protection. However,

---

2. Other relevant international conferences include the International Conference on Population and Development (Cairo 1994); the World Summit for Social Development (Copenhagen 1994 and Copenhagen +5 2000); the Fourth World Conference on Women (1995) and Beijing +5 (2000); the World Food Summit (1996); Habitat II (1996); and the World Conference Against Racism, Racial Discrimination, Xenophobia and Related Intolerance (2001).

while these are necessary steps to fulfilling their obligations, they are not sufficient. Although a state's capacity to legislate and execute policy change and to enforce positive actions through its judicial system are important factors (DFID 2000a), so is political power. States often fulfill their obligations only after being pressured to do so by rights holders. This requires not only agreement on stakeholder

---

BOX 2. KEY NORMATIVE PRINCIPLES

Human freedom: Expanding human freedom entails expanding human liberties, opportunities, and capabilities. Deprivations in human freedom entail not only the denial of civil and political liberties, but also are associated with hunger, poverty, untreated illnesses, and premature mortality. A human rights perspective highlights the importance of processes and policies that expand human freedoms and capabilities by respecting, protecting, and fulfilling individual choices and enabling people to achieve what they value.

Universalism and equality: Human rights are inclusive in character and apply to all people everywhere on an equal basis. This principle recognizes the equal dignity and worth of all human beings. All people should be treated fairly and in a consistent and equitable manner.

The multi-dimensional character of well-being: Human rights for the life, survival, integrity, and development of the person include rights to liberty, security, and well-being. These rights reflect the principles of interdependence and indivisibility in the sense that achievement of all human rights should be given equal priority and urgent consideration.

Transparency, participation, and empowerment: In order to expand freedoms and capabilities, development processes and policies must respect human rights and entitlements. The principles of transparency, participation, and empowerment can help to ensure that development institutions are responsible and accountable, and that people are fully informed, influential, and vested in the decision-making processes that affect their lives.

Responsibility and accountability: Individuals, organizations, and governments have responsibilities to respect, promote, and fulfill all human rights for all. Governments have particular responsibilities and are accountable for respecting, promoting, and fulfilling internationally recognized human rights obligations.

Source: Moser and Norton 2001.

responsibilities to deliver rights, but also the identification of both institutions and policies that can ensure transparency and accountability in implementation (CDS 2002). Finally, while international human rights are obviously of great importance, they are nevertheless only one of a number of rights regimes.

Ushering Rights into International Development Debates, Policies, and Practices

When examining the incorporation of human rights into development, it is useful to start by distinguishing between human rights *per se*, and human rights as an approach to development policy, often called a rights-based approach to development. In the latter, human rights joins a long list of analytical and operational approaches to development (primarily macroeconomic in nature) including modernization, meeting basic needs, neo-liberal structural adjustment, and empowerment. As with other approaches, the origins of rights-based approaches are multiple. Eyben (2003), for instance, identifies the following streams of rights-based thought and practice:

- The international legal human rights framework, a set of United Nations conventions and covenants (discussed above)
- A myriad of social, cultural, and political struggles and debates in both the North and South
- A political science emphasis on the historical evolution of an individual's relation to the state from clientelism to citizenship

Grassroots ownership is recognized in many NGO definitions of rights-based approaches. Save the Children provides one such definition:

> A rights-based approach to development combines human rights, development and social activism to promote justice, equality, and freedom. It makes use of the standards, principles, and approaches of human rights and social activism to address the power issues that lie at the heart of poverty and exploitation in the world. (Save the Children 2003)

As rights-based approaches to development proliferate and multiply—with international institutions, bilateral institutions, and international and national level NGOs all entering the fray—they share a number of common guiding principles that point specifically to the switch from a technical to a political understanding of development.[3] These reiterate the human rights guiding principles mentioned above, adding a particular development spin and including such precepts as the following:

- People are citizens with rights (entitlements and capabilities) rather than beneficiaries with needs.
- The government, with its obligations to its citizens, has a central role to play in rights-based development.
- Grassroots participation is crucial to ensuring that the voices of the poor are heard.

Ultimately, the particular principles of a rights-based approach adopted by an institution may depend as much on internal political factors as it does on differences in technical interpretations of development. Three issues, discussed below, inform our discussion of differences in interpretation.

Sen's Influential Work on Poverty, Freedom, and Rights

Amartya Sen has played a critical role in identifying the linkages between poverty and human rights. In his human rights framework for addressing poverty, he highlights the relevance of freedom and human rights to development. By incorporating the concepts of entitlements, capabilities, opportunities, freedoms, and individual rights into the discourse on poverty, Sen challenges the view that poverty is irrelevant to fundamental freedoms and human rights. Since well-being includes living with substantial freedoms, human development is integrally connected with enhancing certain capabilities, defined as the range of things people can do and be in leading a life (Sen 1999).

Sen spells out the added value of a rights-based approach to development in terms of claims. Examining the commonalities and differences between human development and human rights for the UNDP Human Development Report (2000), he argues that if human development focuses on the enhancements of

---

3. For instance, DFID maintains that the human rights approach to development provides the rationale for empowering people to make their own decisions. DFID's Human Rights Strategy is intended "to enable people to be active citizens with rights, expectations, and responsibilities—based on three cross-cutting principles of participation, inclusion, and fulfilling obligation" (DFID 2000b, 7).

the capabilities and freedoms that the members of a community enjoy, human rights represent the claims that individuals have on the conduct of individual and collective agents, and on the design of social arrangements to facilitate or secure these capabilities and freedoms:

> To have a particular right is to have a claim on other people or institutions that they should help or collaborate in ensuring access to some freedom. This insistence on a claim on others takes us beyond the idea of human development. The normative connection between laudable goals and reasons for actions does not yield specific duties on the part of other individuals, collectivities or social institutions to bring about human development. This is where the human rights approach may offer an additional and very useful perspective for the analysis of human development. It links human development to the idea that others have duties to facilitate and enhance human development. (UNDP 2000, 21)

Building on Sen's work, the UNDP identifies human freedom as the common purpose and motivation of both human rights and human development. While both have distinct traditions and strategies, the two can reinforce each other to expand people's capabilities and to protect their rights and fundamental freedoms (UNDP 2000, 2).

The Right to Development

The UNDP is one of a number of agencies that have advocated for the right to development, which differs in some respects from a rights-based approach to development. The 1986 UN Declaration of the Right to Development notes that "the right to development is an inalienable human right by virtue of which every human person and all peoples are entitled to participate in, contribute to and enjoy economic, social, cultural and political development, in which all human rights and fundamental freedoms can be fully realized" (article 1). States have the duty to take steps, individually and collectively, to formulate international policies with the view to facilitating the full realization of the right. This, the UNDP argues, provides "important guidance in linking norms, processes, and implementation by addressing development as a comprehensive economic, social, and political process" (UNDP 2003, 5).

This position was reinforced by the Millennium Declaration, which states, "We will spare no efforts to free our fellow men, women, and children from the abject and dehumanizing conditions of extreme poverty. We are committed to making the right to development a reality for everyone and to freeing the entire human race from want" (quoted in UNDP 2003, 2).[4]

Some have contested the validity of a right to development on the basis that it is potentially a legally binding claim for some form of global redistributive justice, including claims to aid, debt relief, and fair terms of trade (see Eyben 2003).

> "ULTIMATELY, THE PARTICULAR PRINCIPLES OF A RIGHTS-BASED APPROACH ADOPTED BY AN INSTITUTION MAY DEPEND AS MUCH ON INTERNAL POLITICAL FACTORS AS IT DOES ON DIFFERENCES IN TECHNICAL INTERPRETATIONS OF DEVELOPMENT."

Implicit and Explicit Rights

For the World Bank, the introduction of a rights-based approach to development presents particular challenges. In brief, the Bank's constraints relate historically to its Articles of Agreement, which state that the World Bank must work "with due attention to considerations of economy and efficiency and without regard to political or non-economic influences or considerations" (International Bank for Reconstruction and Development, Articles of Agreement, article III, section 5b).

The Articles of both the IBRD and IDA further state that "the Bank and its officers shall not interfere in the political affairs of any member, nor shall they be influenced in their decisions by the political character of the member or the members concerned. Only economic considerations shall be considered" (IBRD article IV, section 10 and IDA article V, section 6).

However, the Articles do not define what constitutes "economic" as opposed to "political" fields of concern. In his interpretation of the Articles, the Bank's now-retired General Counsel, Ibrahim Shihata, defined a factor as "economic" (and therefore within the Bank's purview) if it had a "direct and obvious" economic effect relevant to the Bank's work (Shihata 1992a, 1992b). In Shihata's interpretation, the Articles of Agreement prevented the World Bank from adopting a rights-based approach to development.

At the same time, the definition as to what counts as a "direct and obvious"

---

4. Building on this, the UNDP has recently identified a human rights-based approach to poverty reduction that identifies as its four key principles: participation and transparency in decision making, non-discrimination, empowerment, and accountability of actors (UNDP 2003, 5).

economic effect has expanded, as the Bank has moved from a narrow focus on growth, through basic needs, poverty reduction, and social services, to recent concerns with environmental protection, gender issues, and civil society participation. This carries the obvious risk that Bank decisions on human rights issues will "appear to be *ad hoc* and somewhat arbitrary" (Bradlow 1996, 79). This was recently illustrated by the *World Development Report 2000/2001*, which identified "facilitating empowerment" as one of three ways to attack poverty and recognized the importance of political processes in development (World Bank 2001, 7).[5]

Building on all of this, of course, is Deepa Narayan's (2002) *Empowerment and Poverty Reduction Sourcebook*'s empowerment framework, which uses language very similar to that used by rights-based approaches. Thus:

1. Empowerment is defined as the expansion of assets and capabilities of poor people to participate in, negotiate with, influence, control, and hold accountable institutions that affect their lives.
2. The empowerment framework identifies as four key elements: information, inclusion/participation, social accountability, and local organizational capacity.
3. It identifies as "analytical linkages," quality of life and human dignity, good governance, pro-poor growth, project effectiveness, and improved service delivery.
4. It also identifies how the framework applies these elements to four critical development objectives: the provision of basic services, improving local and national governance, access to markets, and access to justice.

Prior to this quantum leap in the development of the empowerment approach, the World Bank distinguished between implicit and explicit rights. In its contribution to the 50th anniversary of the Universal Declaration of Human Rights, the Bank argued that because the Bank promotes human rights on a number of fronts and in a number of ways, it need not be explicit in its overarching commitment to the totality of human rights principles (Gaeta and Vasilara 1998).

---

5. The linkages between politics and poverty were explored in commissioned background papers, such as Moore and Putzel (1999).

The Bank makes a second distinction between the indirect and direct promotion of rights, arguing that it promotes human rights indirectly, as economic and social rights are fulfilled through economic growth. It emphasizes that, while development is not possible without human rights, the converse also holds true: human rights are not possible without development. Human rights, then, are the ends but not the means. The Bank promotes human rights *directly*, but in discrete sectors (for example, in its support for participation, judicial reform, accountability, and gender equality). Finally, in a very recent paper, the World Bank succinctly argues the case for the "congruence" between poverty reduction, as defined in the PRSP, and a human rights approach to development (World Bank 2004).

Implementing Rights-Based Approaches: Contestation and Power Relations

While an extensive, rich debate now exists on human rights-based approaches to development at the policy level, evidence for the successful implementation of such approaches—including the way power relations play out in the field—is far more limited. This final section raises a number of related issues.

Changing the Agenda: UNICEF's Experience of Institutional and Technical Constraints

As one of the lead institutions implementing a human rights-based approach to planning (HRBAP), UNICEF has been "operationalizing the paradigm shift from a needs-based to a rights-based approach to development" since the 1998 Executive Directive (UNICEF 1998). Under a traditional needs-based approach, UNICEF primarily provided support to the provision of services at the national, local, and community levels, with local participation in decision making and implementation. Under HRBAP, UNICEF primarily provides assistance to strengthening national and local capacities for effective action in realizing the rights of children and women, for programs and projects requested by and jointly designed and monitored with national partners.

Within Executive Directive's broad guidelines, country offices have considerable autonomy in designing overall strategy and choosing programming priorities. Hence, operationalization has different meanings for country and regional offices across the world. As one of its lead advocates, Urban Jonsson, argues, "In a human rights context, the *processes* by which such goals are achieved are as important as the *outcomes*" (UNICEF ESARO 2001).

Recently, in an effort to systematize diverse interventional practice, UNICEF used a twin-track programming process (United Nations 2003) to distinguish between practices that are essential to HRBAP and practices that are unique to a HRBAP. Regarding practices that are essential to HRBAP, UNICEF's role is to shift from directly supporting service delivery to strengthening national and local capacity, including the capacity for basic service delivery, as duty bearers and rights holders. This requires the introduction of a new perspective into ongoing, long-term UNICEF programming areas.

Regarding practices that are unique to a HRBAP, UNICEF's role *a priori* is to strengthen national and local capacity of duty bearers and rights holders. In other words, activities are based on collaboration with national and local counterparts. An example of such activities is providing support for the use of participatory processes to draft legislation.

While the twin-track programming over-simplifies the complexity of a HRBAP, it is nevertheless a useful tool to analyze trends, highlight constraints, and identify important ways to strengthen a HRBAP. One interesting challenge identified in a recent assessment relates to the language of accountability and ownership. Country reports consistently discuss activities and programs as if UNICEF were the owner, though its role is to assist and support government, CSOs, and local communities as the rightful owners of such activities. Many of UNICEF's country offices must still work diligently to change their language (Moser and Moser 2003).

Power and Implementation

In seeking to integrate an understanding of the ways in which power acts as a development variable, particularly how the negotiating capabilities of poor people can be strengthened in the face of prevailing structures of power and authority, Moser and Norton (2001) identify a framework that operates at the following three levels, each with associated analytical tools:

Normative level: This element relies on international standards of equity, transparency, inclusion, and participation to identify human rights from the top down. As described above, the value added of building explicitly on human rights as a basis for operational practice is based on the global legitimacy of human rights acquired through extensive international discussion, negotiation, and agreement. While such processes were originally predominantly governmental, they have been strengthened considerably by heavy civil society involvement in the big UN conferences of the 1990s.

Analytical level: This element elaborates the ways in which poor people's claims are processed into outcomes by multiple structures of authority and control, which operate at different levels. Analysis targets the associated social and political processes that determine the likelihood of poor people's claims being reflected in the definition, interpretation, or implementation of rights. This level also seeks to identify the social characteristics (gender, citizenship, social status, ethnicity, and the like) that empower or disempower people in different arenas of negotiation.

Methodologies and tools at the analytical level must incorporate a better understanding of the way that power affects the production and reproduction of poverty and insecurity. These include, first, a rights regime analysis, which identifies rights regimes at different levels with associated domains and operational or authority structures (see appendix 1). Second, methodology and tools must include a channel of contestation matrix, which identifies various institutional channels through which claims can be contested (political, legal, policy, administrative, social, and private sectors), the types of claims that relate to each institutional domain, and the method of citizen action that can be used to make those claims (see appendix 2).

Operational level: This level explores the ways in which a focus on rights can be used to identify new and significant entry points for the actions of development agencies, governments, and civil society actors who seek to strengthen poor people's capacity to reduce their poverty through greater livelihood security. Although many of the entry points may appear similar to those for poverty reduction more generally, there is a difference in the way that a rights perspective illuminates the linkages between different levels of intervention. For example, a PRSP can help initiate discussions about allocating monies to support poor people's access to justice (see Norton and Elson 2002), policy priorities, and the role of the legal system in facilitating access to, and securing tenure of, key assets. The originality of a rights perspective is that it highlights the linkages between different arenas.

By combining the normative and analytical components with operations, a rights-based approach can help development agencies incorporate empowerment goals into their work in concrete ways.

Rights in Principle, Rights in Practice

In practice, negotiations over rights can be seen as arenas of contestation in which structures of power and authority are manifested. A rights-based approach allows us to identify the ways in which contestation is context specific. Entry points for negotiation depend on a range of factors. For example, the Millennium Development Goal of environmental sustainability intends "by 2020 to achieve significant improvement in the lives of at least 100 million slum dwellers." Urban land tenure is pertinent to that target. Land rights are essential to ensure the quality and security of homes and neighborhoods (Satterthwaite 2003). Further, possessing land rights is a precondition to acquiring other assets that support livelihoods, such as establishing a home-based enterprise, renting out rooms in the home to augment income, and having collateral for credit, all of which are linked to poverty reduction among slum dwellers (Moser 1998).

The following two very different experiences in claiming rights to land tenure highlight the fact that while top-down laws and legal frameworks may provide an important normative basis on which to claim rights, in practice, bottom-up mobilization and local advocacy campaigns may be necessary to achieve success in the contestation of claims.

The first example from Guayaquil, Ecuador, illustrates the limitations of normative frameworks in practice. In this Latin American city, squatter's rights to land on the peripheral low-land mangrove *suburbios* were decreed some 30 years ago by a 1974 Municipal Ordinance, which required the municipality to give existing squatters titles to plots (*solars*), provided that the person had resided there at least a year, owned no other land in the city, and that the plot was no larger than 300 square meters in size. The ordinance established the Office for the Distribution of *Solars* to allocate and administer titles to the land (Moser 1982).

Yet, some 30 years later a considerable proportion of the original squatters still have not completed the process necessary to obtain a legal deed (*escritura*). A recently completed 1978-1992-2004 panel data set of some 47 households showed that, while households know their rights and acknowledge the importance of obtaining deeds, the majority of eligible households have failed to complete the process. This appears inexplicable until one examines the complexity, time, and costs of the process.

According to local community members, as table 1 shows, obtaining a deed involves up to ten different steps. At each step, a household must acquire a range of legal documents. Further, the costs of completing the process are often prohibitive. While the process purportedly costs the equivalent of two to three months' minimum salary ($343) at the lowest level, according to community

TABLE 1. STEPS IN OBTAINING LEGAL DEED FOR LAND TITLE IN THE SUBURBIOS
OF GUAYAQUIL, AS PERCEIVED BY COMMUNITY MEMBERS

Step	Process	Issuing Institutions	Cost in theory (in dollars)	Actual cost (in dollars)
1	**Legalization** *Documents required:* • Certificate of identity of household head and spouse, if married.	Dept. of Civil Registration	6	15-20
	• Certificate of voting of household head and spouse, if married.	Electoral tribunal	6	15-20
	-Make solicitude -Measure plot size -Submit social and technical report on family situation	Dept. of Land, Municipality	free	100-300
2	**Purchase of Document of Estimation of Legalization**	Municipal Office (*Ventanillo*)	5	5
3	**Register property to prove that one does not own any other plot** *Documents required:*	Office of Registration of Property (previously the Palace of Justice)	15	30
	• Certificate of identity of all adult household members	Dept. of Civil Registration	6 per adult	15-20 per adult
4	**Pull all documents in a yellow folder with band (*bincha*)** *Documents required:* • All noted in step 1 above	Legalization Office, Dept of Land, Municipality	15-20	20-30
	• Birth certificate of all sons and daughters	Dept. of Civil Registration	5 per child	5 per child
5	**Obtain municipal approval in three council sessions (these take place before elections and at the Annual Festival of Guayaquil)**	Dept. of Land, Municipal	-	-

(continued)

Step	Process	Issuing Institutions	Cost in theory (in dollars)	Actual cost (in dollars)
6	Pay the value of the plot and confirm that the fee has been registered	Central Bank	10-30 (depends on plot size)	30
7	Send the minutes of the award to the notary/ Notarize the deed	Notary Office of the Canton	200	200
8	Write to the Property Registration Dept.	Property Registration Dept.	50	50
9	Buy Evaluation of Value in Kind (*especie valorado*)	Department of Catastral Survey, Municipality	5-10	10-15
10	Take the completed documentation to the Dept. of Catastral Survey	Department of Catastral Survey, Municipality	-	-
Total			$363*	$745

*Minimum for 2 adult, 1 child household
Source: Moser 2004.

members, actual costs may total six months' minimum salary ($745) because some personnel must be paid to ensure the process is completed. Hernando de Soto (2000) has written extensively about the South American legal system as a development constraint, and a human-rights perspective shows that the poor are particularly disempowered. A legal framework does not ensure access in practice since individual households are often incapable of successfully negotiating their way through this complex legal labyrinth.

In contrast to the squatters' experience with the legal system in Guayaquil is the recent—and proliferating—success of urban squatter associations and alliances in 11 countries in the South, including India, Zimbabwe, Thailand, and the Philippines. These associations have their roots in community-based saving groups, but they are not small community-level NGOs or CBOs; they are extensive national-level federations formed by urban poor groups to give themselves the necessary leverage for the successful contestation of claims (Appaduri 2001) (see box 3).

In South Africa, for example, over 100,000 people living in shacks and rented rooms in formal and informal settlements are members of the South African Homeless People's Federation. They have secured land for over 20,000 families and have financed directly the construction of over 10,000 houses. Similarly, the Philippines Homeless People's Federation has over 20,000 members based in different cities. All are saving money and seeking ways to

---

Box 3. Urban poor federations claiming rights through processes of "bottom-up contestation"

Since 1990, slum and shack dwellers in Asia, South Africa, and elsewhere have formed federations and supported a gradually expanding program of direct, community-to-community exchanges aimed at transforming the lives and livelihoods of urban poor populations. This movement of federations, known as Shack/Slum Dwellers International (SDI), has grown to include over 650,000 people in 11 countries.

Federations are changing the ways urban poverty is addressed by demonstrating new ways to:

- implement projects, including their own housing and infrastructure, with much lower costs and better quality than government projects.
- develop grassroots organizations that are controlled by and accountable to member households. Most federations have at their base savings groups formed primarily by low-income women.
- learn from and support one other through community-to-community exchange between savings groups in each city, as well as nationally and internationally, and help establish new federations.
- influence policy by setting successful precedence and using this to negotiate changes in policy. The federations have legitimacy by being large and representative and by demonstrating feasible, cost-effective solutions.
- develop their own knowledge base through undertaking their own surveys and censuses.
- influence the policies and priorities of international agencies through their own international organization, SDI.

What makes SDI different from other transnational citizen networks is that the locus of power and authority is kept in communities themselves rather than in intermediary NGOs at national or international levels. This is partly because SDI was set up to promote practical solidarity, mutual support, and the exchange of useful information among their members about development strategies and concrete alternatives.

Sources: IIED 2001, Edwards 2001.

develop their homes through negotiating for secure land, forming homeowners associations, identifying sites where they can build homes, and exploring sources for loans (VMSDFI 2001).

Concluding Comment

This paper briefly outlines the ways in which a human rights approach is gradually being mainstreamed, either directly or indirectly, into the work of development agencies. Given the close linkages between rights and power, mainstreaming rights-based approaches means that such institutions are also increasingly incorporating issues of power and power relations into their dialogue and practice. The critical importance of this shift in focus and the recognition that development is a highly political process is best illustrated by increasingly active, politically motivated social movements, organized around basic needs such as housing, water, and livelihood-related resources. Their sophisticated understanding of the political nature of development practice shows how far these groups have already come towards using contestation as a means to claim rights, rather than relying on negotiation for the top-down delivery of essential services.

References

Appadurai, Arjun 2001. Deep democracy: Urban governmentality and the horizons of politics. *Environment and Urbanization* 13 (2): 23–43.

Bradlow, D. 1996. The World Bank, the IMF, and human rights. *Transnational Law and Contemporary Problems* 47 (6): 47–90.

CDS. 2002. PRAMS: Linking participation and institutional change. Working paper. Glasgow: Centre for Development Studies, Swansea and Edinburgh Resource Centre.

De Soto, Hernando. 2000. *The mystery of capitalism: Why capitalism triumphs in the West and fails everywhere else.* New York: Basic Books.

DFID. 2000a. Making government work for poor people. Target strategy paper. London: Department for International Development.

———. 2000b. Realising human rights for poor people. Target strategy paper. London: Department for International Development.

Edwards, Michael 2001. Global civil society and community exchanges: A different form of movement. *Environment and Urbanization* 13 (2): 145-149.

Eyben, Rosalind. 2003. *The rise of rights: Rights-based approaches to international development*. IDS Policy Briefing Issue 17. Brighton, UK: Institute of Development Studies.

Gaeta, Anthony and Marina Vasilara. 1998. *Development and human rights: The role of the World Bank*. Washington, DC: World Bank.

IIED. 2001. *Environment and Urbanization Brief* 4. London: International Institute of Environment and Development.

Moore, Mick, and James Putzel. 1999. Thinking strategically about politics and poverty. IDS Working Paper No. 101. Brighton, UK: Institute of Development Studies.

Moser, Caroline. 1982. A home of one's own: Squatter housing strategies in Guayaquil, Ecuador. In *Urbanization in Contemporary Latin America*. Eds. A. Gilbert and R. Ramirez. London: Wiley.

———. 1998. The asset vulnerability framework: Reassessing urban poverty reduction strategies. *World Development* 26 (1): 1–19.

———. 2004. Unpublished Guayaquil field notes.

Moser, Caroline, and Annalise Moser. 2003. Moving ahead with human rights: Assessment of the operationalization of the human rights based approach in UNICEF programming: 2002, UNICEF Evaluation Paper.

Moser, Caroline, and Andy Norton. 2001. *To claim our rights: Livelihood security, human rights and sustainable development*. London: Overseas Development Institute.

Narayan, Deepa. 2002. Introduction. *Empowerment and poverty reduction: A sourcebook*. Ed. Deepa Narayan. Washington, DC: World Bank.

Norton, Andy. 2001. Background paper on rights regimes. Mimeo. London: Overseas Development Institute.

Norton, Andy, and Diane Elson. 2002. *What's behind the budget: Politics, rights and accountability in the budget process*. London: Overseas Development Institute.

Satterthwaite, David, ed. 2003. *The Millennium Development Goals and local processes: Hitting the target or missing the point?* London: International Institute for Environment and Development.

Sen, Amartya. 1999. *Development as freedom*. Oxford: Oxford University Press.

Shihata, Ibrahim F. I. 1992a. The World Bank and human rights: An analysis of the legal issues and the record of achievements. *Denver Journal of International Law and Policy* 17: 39–66.

———. 1992b. Human rights, development and international financial institutions. *American University Journal of International Law and Policy* (8): 35–45.

UNDP. 2000. *Human development report 2000: Human rights and human development.* New York: Oxford University Press.

———. 2003. *Poverty reduction and human rights: A practical note.* New York: UNDP.

UNICEF. 1998. Guidelines for human-rights based programming approach. Executive Directive. CF/EXD/1998-04. New York: UNICEF.

UNICEF ESARO. 2001. Operationalization for ESAR of UNICEF global guidelines for human rights programming. Nairobi: UNICEF ESARO.

United Nations. 2003. *The human rights based approach to development cooperation: Towards a common understanding among the UN agencies.* Geneva: United Nations.

Vizard, Polly. 2001. Human rights and development: Evolving international agendas. Background paper. London: Overseas Development Institute.

Vincentian Missionaries Social Development Foundation Incorporated (VMSDFI). 2001. Meet the Philippines Homeless People's Foundation, *Environment and Urbanization* 13 (2): 73–84.

World Bank. 2001. *World development report 2000/2001: Attacking poverty.* Washington, DC: World Bank.

———. 2004a. *Human rights and the poverty reduction strategy paper approach.* Paper presented by Gobind Nankani at the Ethical Globalization Initiative and the NYU Center for Human Rights and Global Justice conference Human Rights and Development: Towards Mutual Reinforcement.

———. 2004b. Social development in World Bank operations: Results and way forward. Discussion paper. Washington, DC: World Bank.

Appendix 1. Rights Regimes Analysis

Social and Political Contestation	Rights regime	Forms of rights and domain	Level of operational/ institutional framework and authority structures	Legal and Administrative Implementation
↑ ... Livelihood and social groups seeking to make claims on the means for sustainable livelihoods. Capacity to make claims and influence rights regimes depends on social identity and the authority and power that this confers ---e.g. gender, caste, class.	International human rights law	Human Rights (economic, social, cultural, political, legal, civil, labor standards). Universal application.	International, Global level. Implemented and monitored through UN inter-government processes.	Rights regimes implemented through the operation of the legal system and the allocation of resources and administration of services
	Regional law	Human Rights (as above). Applies to regional populations.	International, Regional level. Increasingly with statutory powers of enforcement, e.g., European Court of Human Rights.	
	Constitutional law	National Constitutional rights (mostly civil and political but starting to include economic and social through influence of human rights, e.g., South Africa).	National level. Enforced through constitutional courts, national legal mechanisms.	
	Statutory law	Statutory rights (conferred by the national framework of criminal, commercial and other law).	National or local level (through devolved local government enacting by-laws). Enforced through formal legal system.	
	Religious law	Religious rights and norms (mostly operating in the domestic sphere; under some conditions considerably extended).	Religious systems of law can operate at multiple levels: global, regional, national, and local. Forms of authority and enforcement depend on relation with the state.	
	Customary Law	Customary Right (mostly referring to kinship and resource rights) Specific to localities and social/ethnic groups.	Local level (generally in colonial or post-colonial states only). Enforced through structures of customary authority (e.g., chiefs)	
	Living Law	Informal right (mostly kinship and resource rights) and norms of behavior. Applies to localities through varying cultures (including institutional cultures).	Micro level. No formal incorporation into national legal systems. Nonetheless, local elites may be able to co-opt elements of the state to help enforce elements of living law. Living law can also be taken as describing the norms of behavior operating within bureaucracies (governments, donor agencies).	↓

Source: Moser and Norton 2001.

Appendix 2. Channels of Contestation Matrix

Institutional Channel	Types of claim	Method of citizen action
Political system	Processes of identifying new rights and securing changes to formally recognized freedoms and entitlements, such as the women's movement demand for recognition of reproductive rights. Negotiations over how rights and entitlements should be interpreted and recognized. Negotiations over how entitlements should be implemented, such as through private or public sector provision.	• Voting in formal elections and referenda (national and local) • Lobbying for change through representational system • Open struggle • Media reporting and information provision • Public hearings, e.g. South Africa Poverty Hearings • Open advocacy (intermediate groups acting on behalf of people seeking to assert claims) use of media and campaigning • Informal and invisible advocacy through contacts, such as interactions with sympathetic officials
Legal system	Process of interpretation and implementation of legally recognized rights, often relating to physical, natural, and financial assets (such as land), but also social assets (such as marital relations) and human assets (such as education and health-related claims).	• Legal action and challenge at local, national, and international levels (claims to land rights, disputes over forced evictions, cases around domestic disputes and violence, and bankruptcy) • Engagement with law enforcement agencies; disputes may be settled through local police rather than the courts • Appeal to arbitration and monitoring services, such as human rights commissions, ombudspersons, industrial tribunals, and arbitration services, which monitor and regulate public services and private sector standards • Engagement in formal human rights treaty monitoring processes (state reports to Treaty Monitoring Bodies)
Policy channels	Negotiation over interpretation of public provision of entitlements, often most directly relating to human assets, for example, provision of public services.	• Engagement in international policy processes, such as the conferences in Rio and Beijing • Engagement in policy and planning processes at national and local levels, such as PRSPs, SWAps, and local governance planning often about public service priorities such as levels and quality of health and education provision • Engagement in defining and monitoring budget processes and resource allocation for policy priorities; participatory budgeting
Administrative channels	Negotiation over interpretation and implementation of entitlements, often relating to human and social assets.	• Individual claims on resources and services, for example, everyday interactions with health workers • Collective monitoring of public services and provision, such as report cards, citizen service groups, benchmarking, monitoring codes of conduct, social audits
Social channels	Negotiation over access to natural resources (for example, land) and social resources (for example, labor).	• Informal negotiation over entitlements to resources • Informal debates about gender roles and responsibilities, including the evolution of the conditions of the marital contract
Private sector channels	Negotiation over interpretation and implementation of private sector related entitlements, often relating to human assets, for example, labor rights and access to financial assets.	• Union and civil society action over labor standards and collective bargaining for wages with employees • Engagement with banks and other organizations to ensure credit provision • Engagement in defining and monitoring voluntary codes of conduct • Consumer action such as boycotting products or monitoring quality of services • Shareholder action

4. Power Relations and Poverty Reduction

David Mosse, School of Oriental and African Studies, University of London

For many reasons, the concept of power has attracted relatively little attention in policy analysis among international development agencies. And yet, power has been central to the frameworks that inform academic social science; emphasized, perhaps, to a fault.[1] Nonetheless, power, disempowerment, and empowerment are increasingly part of the analysis of poverty and its alleviation, and inequality in power relations is taken to explain important constraints to poverty reduction measures.

Power inequalities inhere in interpersonal relations and in the community. They are part of the dynamics among beneficiaries, development agencies, and the state, and can be found in the hierarchies of organizations as well as in interagency and donor-client relations. The effects of power relations on poverty reduction are many. The interests of national elites and the electoral concerns of those in power affect the state's policy choices, sector priorities, and programs, with important consequences for the poor. Equally, well-intentioned sector reform programs can run aground where they challenge vested interests, and democratic reforms often have limited or unpredictable effect on power relations. And where local elites are well placed to capture benefits and reservations (in education, employment, or for elections), or to manipulate the

---

1. Sahlins (1999, 404) takes to task the "afterologists" who end up knowing everything only "functionally, as devices of power...not substantially or structurally."

administrative system upon which the poor depend for their livelihood and for access to anti-poverty schemes, formal processes of decentralization may do little to reduce informal forces of domination (Jenkins 2002).

Power is pervasive; it is not just structure, but also the electrical current of society. In this paper I want to set out some ways of thinking about power, and then look at some different approaches to empowerment within development. In various ways these approaches attempt to address the effects of power inequalities on the achievement of poverty reduction goals.

Conceptualizing Power

Concepts of power vary widely, ranging from Weber's (1964) pluralistic notion of the command of force to Foucault's (1980) discourses of truth and knowledge. Indeed, thinking about power relations, empowerment, and poverty requires a broad framework. For present purposes, it may help to draw six preliminary distinctions.

First, formal and legitimate forms of power, such as government councils, the police, and so on, can be distinguished from informal, dispersed, or, in Foucault's terms, "capillary" power. Of course, formal power can be distinguished in terms of the different sources from which it is derived (or legitimized); for example, the power of bureaucratic authority versus the power of popular approval (Weber's rational legal versus charismatic authority). When thinking about empowerment, however, it is as important to think about the relationship between such formal authority and informal relations of power. It is well known that the operation of formal structures is underpinned by informal relations, and it is the hope of reform agendas that formal processes (policy, decentralization, structures of representation) will have an impact on unequal, informal power relations (for example, democratic decentralization on inter-caste relations in India).

Second, analyses of power can be distinguished in terms of whether they emphasize the modes of domination from "the top," or the everyday exercise of power at "the bottom." Of course, power can be analyzed at many different levels.

Third, sometimes power is conceptualized as infinitely expanding and augmented by economic growth; but at other times as finite, as a scarce resource like land, water, or state resources over which groups compete (Cheater 1999). The latter is a zero-sum view of power that Moore and Putzel (1999) characterize as "interest group economism." This distinction is related to that between the promotion of *power to* do various things, and competition for *power over* things or people (Nelson and Wright 1994).

Fourth, there is a distinction between *actor-oriented* and *structural* views of power. In actor-oriented or transactionalist (Weberian) views, power is a non-economic resource that individuals seek to maximize, rather as they might maximize economic returns. Power is subject to rational choice, and ways of strategically maximizing power can be modeled (for example, Bailey 1969, in Gledhill 1994). Other actor-focused analysts are more interested in the goals, interests, and unequal effects of power plays, such as the uneven accumulation of political capital, or profit, in the form of symbolic or cultural capital, prestige, honor, or popularity (Bourdieu 1977). Political capital allows certain groups in society privileged access to public resources, whether public works contracts or jobs within an administrative service (cf. Wade 1982). But political capital is also necessary for the poor, whose rights and assets have to be negotiated and defended politically (Baumann 2000). In economistic formulations, political capital is regarded as an asset that links individuals or groups to the power structure (ibid).

A problem with viewing power in terms of individual or group strategies is that it does not explain the systematic nature of social behavior (Gledhill 1994). Symbolic and political capital are closely related to the accumulation of economic capital and the reproduction of class structures, but it is also a matter of the effects of these on individual behavior. People's behavior is conditioned by durable dispositions (cognitive and behavioral) derived from historical forces and "tend[s] to reproduce the regularities immanent in the objective conditions," which Bourdieu terms *habitus* (1977, 78, in Gledhill 1994).[2] This is a useful concept, not least because it indicates the complex subjective and objective demands of empowerment. For example, those working to empower socially subordinated groups like the Dalits in India explain that their work involves changing assumed meanings and entrenched habits by initiating a process of re-socialization, in which individuals learn through practice to modify the distinctions and schemes that produced their disempowerment, as

---

2. Here, Bourdieu offers a theory which addresses an issue that is left unresolved in social capital studies (especially in the weak modeling of causal mechanisms in econometric analyses of the relation between social capital and poverty indicators), namely, what constitutes a social influence on individual behavior (Durlauf 2002).

well as to achieve economic independence (Arun 2004). There are parallels with work on gender relations. It is significant that activists often see conflict, even violence, as necessary to disrupt old meanings, and education as necessary to produce new ones. Of course, unequal power relations are naturalized as habits and classifications to different degrees, so opportunities for change and reactions to it vary in different cultural contexts. The violent retaliation to efforts to change unequal relations between upper castes and Dalits (evident in atrocities against Dalits), or to change gender relations (evident in links between domestic violence and micro-finance initiatives)[3] demonstrates a strongly embedded habitus.

Opposing actor-focused positions is the idea of power as structure, which has a strong tradition in social science. Of course, such structures are not visible; rather, they are *ideas* about the distribution or balance of power in a given society (Leach 1964). The idea of a power structure usually makes sense only in relation to other things such as the distribution of land, wealth, or other assets. The idea of a power structure also depends upon the cultural construction of power, which varies from society to society. For example, the relationship between religious, political, and economic power or status is not constant. Much scholarly ink has been spilt on this issue.[4] The idea of a power structure that defines individuals and groups by their position in the socioeconomic order can offer a rather static view. Indeed, generally speaking, structural theories that explain the reproduction of power relations are not so good at explaining *change* in power structures (Gledhill 1994). But power structures and the institutions through which they are expressed are indeed profoundly changed by historical circumstances.[5] For example, introducing landed property rights in many colonial settings where power derived from the control over people rather than over assets (or from redistribution rather than production) had profound

---

3. Micro-finance initiatives can also have the opposite effect of reducing domestic violence, for example in adivasi western India, by morally delegitimizing existing forms of social capital mediated by alcohol (see Mosse 2004a, 216–7).

4. See, for example, the debates on secular power and religious status in India opened up by Louis Dumont's work (1980).

5. My own work in south India (Mosse 2003a) shows that it is not just inequality or the concentration of power and authority that is relevant for social outcomes, but also how power is articulated: whether for example through public institutions (such as temples and water systems) or through more diffuse private networks of patronage, alliance, and personal obligation.

implications for the structure of power relations at local and regional levels. Similarly, the shift to a market economy and a new power of money in relation to institutions and office in post-Soviet societies also had transforming effects on power relations. The world over, structures of power have been changed in regionally and locally specific ways by universal franchise and electoral politics that give a new power in numbers, and which can also unleash populist violence turned on "market-dominant minorities" (Chua 2003).

In a fifth conception of power, unequal power relations are more or less concealed from those whose lives are shaped by them. Some theorists stress the idea of a hegemony of the powerful, the domination or oppression of minds and aspirations, and the production of a "false consciousness" among subordinate groups who appear to be in consensus with systems that oppress them. Other theorists emphasize the agency and everyday resistance of the poor, such as Scott's (1985) many "weapons of the weak," as well as the more overt forms of rebellion or conflict.

Finally, power can be understood as political representation. In this case, power does not concern only people's actions and relations, but also the language, classifications, and organizations through which they are represented as interests and groups within political systems (Gledhill 1994). The point here is that power relations in society are always shaped by wider political systems. The power that people have (as individuals and groups) depends upon the capacity of others (for example, labor union leaders and party workers) to impose social classifications upon them and then speak on their behalf. It is the process of classification that "turns the group from a collection of individuals to a political force" (ibid. 139).[6] In this view, political parties or organizations do not reflect any naturally occurring classes, castes, ethnicities, and the like, but rather manufacture these categories through the process of determining who gets political representation. The party precedes the class struggle. Further, the political system is a professionalized field in which political capital is held in the hands of a few (ibid).

---

6. "The fact that the working classes are widely deemed to exist is based on their political representation by political and trade union apparatuses and party officials 'who have a vital interest in believing that this class exists and in spreading this belief among those who consider themselves part of it as well as those who are excluded from it'" (Bourdieu 1991, 250; quoted in Gledhill 1994, 139).

Empowerment and the Poor

Next, I want to identify some of the different approaches to empowerment as a means to poverty reduction, which draw on these different ideas of power.

Capacity Building vs. Struggle

Voluntaristic approaches to empowerment emphasize training, awareness raising, and capacity building for individuals and groups. Power here is the *power to* achieve ends. It is an infinitely expanding resource, but its conception is often limited to "having a place, a voice, [and] being represented within administrative or managerial systems" (James 1999, 14). Empowering organizations make the most of their staff potential (ibid). However, critics suggest that this sort of empowerment may be linked to restructuring, downsizing, cost-cutting, and flattening management structures. In this sense, it can be antithetical to acquiring political power through collective bargaining or union action (ibid), and may even strengthen the power of managers, bosses, and owners. In contrast to *power to* is a view of empowerment as struggle for *power over* resources (or other people), often within a zero-sum game in which the rich and the poor, managers and workers, are opponents. The "interest group economism" (Moore and Putzel 1999) that promotes this view of empowerment is in turn criticized for its failure to see the coalitions and mutual interests between rich and poor, state and citizens, that can sustain pro-poor agendas (see below).

Anti-Poverty Programs vs. Decentralized Democracy

There are many NGO and state-run community-driven development interventions that have an empowerment agenda as part of specific programs. Such projects aim to empower from the bottom up through participative planning, technology development, and the promotion of self-help groups or users' associations for improved management of resources such as water, forests, grazing land, finance, public utilities, and the like. The potential of such programs to enhance poor people's *power to* achieve their ends is rarely in question. Real needs and interests are addressed through resource user associations, which are more accessible and inclusive than elite-dominated systems of local government. The need for poor people to form associations to contend with the power of the rich, or as a means to deal with injustice, formed the core of NGO strategies in South Asia from the early 1980s.

However, the capacity of such interventions to overcome rather than reproduce wider unequal power relations is also questioned. Development programs and their user groups can operate in ways that limit poor people's potential to enhance their political capabilities or to sustain political organization, and may actually demobilize existing organizations (Moore and Putzel 1999). Significantly, such a critical position is taken both by those who favor operating within state systems and those who favor working against the state; by those who prefer to work through formal politics as well as by those who operate through extra-political mass action. Let me illustrate the point.

Numerous rural development initiatives undertaken in India in the 1990s, including DFID's rainfed farming projects and the GOI's watershed development programs, aimed to empower the poor, especially through mobilizing the grassroots for the management of key livelihood resources. However, these initiatives have been subject to criticism in terms of their capacity to address power relations.

For one thing, the village-level associations they promote tend to be dominated by the more affluent and powerful members of society, especially since they are avenues to the important material and political resources of outside agencies. Kumar and Corbridge (2002) argue that the effect of such programs is not only to concentrate local power, but also to weaken existing institutions of collective action (grain banks, reciprocal labor) that offer some livelihood security to the poorest of the poor. Moreover, NGOs and other implementing agencies tend to develop clientalist relationships with their villager beneficiaries, who, as individuals or self-help groups, are willing recipients of efficiently delivered programs (Mosse 2004a). So development interventions, even those with explicit agendas of participation, community-driven development, or empowerment, tend to affirm power structures; they tend to be inherently conservative, reconstituting rather than challenging relations of power, authority, and patronage at every level—in target villages (between landlords and labor), in the project teams, or within the corporate organization, donor, and beyond (cf. Harriss 2002).

These unequal power relations can shape the very instruments that are intended to be empowering. Thus, in "participatory planning" outsider expert perspectives win over local knowledge, needs and plans being determined with reference to outsider agendas, and local organizations develop as dependent client bodies seeking patronage. The concern with strengthening demand occurs in the context of supply. This means that despite the ideals of participation, "people become empowered not in themselves, but through relationships with outsiders; and not through the validation of their existing knowledge and actions, but by seeking out and acknowledging the superiority of modern technology and lifestyles, and by aligning themselves with dominant cultural forms" (Mosse 2004a, 218; cf. Fiedrich 2002).

Project structures entail a degree of uncertainty, arbitrariness, inequality, and patronage, which does not provide an environment in which collective action by the poor is encouraged. Moreover, these development programs are invariably implemented through non-state Project Implementing Agencies; they establish authorities against which rights cannot be asserted (cf. Moore and Putzel 1999, 16).

The empowerment credentials of Indian state anti-poverty programs that aim to transfer resources management from state bureaucracies to user communities are hardly better. User groups in India, are often regarded as undemocratic, unaccountable, and easily controlled or manipulated by the departmental bureaucracies that promote them, and as unlikely to be sustained or to foster wider forms of organization among the poor. Typically, the powers and rights that poor people acquire through them are heavily circumscribed, especially by lower level bureaucrats (Manor 2002). This is not to say that transferring resource management does not have effects on power relations (e.g., by making new demands on officials), merely that their effects are not systematically in favor of the poor. Precisely because they threaten powerful interests in the bureaucracy, user groups may be controlled, resisted, or resented. In south Indian irrigation, for example, there is an unconstructive stalemate. While irrigation officers have little to gain and much to lose from increased accountability to water users associations (WUAs) under participatory irrigation management—that is, their capacity to benefit personally from increasing risk and rent seeking through privileged knowledge is reduced—farmers organizations themselves have no formal means of holding officials accountable. "And although WUAs have little authority and no legal right to manage irrigation systems, their existence, and the links which they are able to forge with politicians and senior levels in the bureaucracy, still signal a de-motivating loss of power to officials within state level irrigation bureaucracies" (Mosse 2003a, 291).

Many studies suggest that the evidence on the long-term sustainability of user groups, especially with the removal of external incentives, is equivocal—even in the case of groups supported intensively by NGOs, some for as many as seven to ten years (Saxena 2001). Of course there are other studies that show

how new user groups can be routes to empowerment; for instance, challenging existing social exclusions of lower castes from resources. Associations may also preserve indigenous institutional arrangements (as well as erode them). One thing is clear: without longitudinal studies it is impossible to predict the longer-term effects of new associations.

Now, a view that commands growing support among policymakers is that the poor will be empowered not through central anti-poverty programs, but through the process of political decentralization that devolves resources and decision making to elected local councils, such as Panchyati raj institutions in India. Indeed, the strongest critics of centrally controlled programs and their users' associations and self-help groups (SHGs) in India are often the greatest supporters of political decentralization and Panchayati raj as the best route to empowerment of the poor (Manor 2002). They argue that the indiscriminate promotion of well-resourced user committees and other parallel bodies undermines the processes of democratic decentralization and diverts resources from elected bodies, which is detrimental to the long-term interests of the poor. Problems include the overlapping of jurisdiction, confusion and the usurpation of roles and functions, a fragmentation of popular participation, and the balkanizing of accountability to diverse programs, departments, and donors (ibid).

However, some research suggests that democratic decentralization itself may fail to change unequal power relations in favor of the poor, while bureaucratically managed program delivery may actually be more effective at enhancing their political capabilities.

The Politics of Governance and Poverty Reduction: the Case of Madhya Pradesh and Andhra Pradesh

Different state governments in India have emphasized to different degrees the promotion of anti-poverty programs and user groups and democratic decentralization. There is an interesting comparison between the state of Madhya Pradesh (MP), which officially launched a radical program of political decentralization, and Andhra Pradesh (AP) which devolved powers to a lesser extent and adopted a populist approach to poverty reduction through line departments and parallel bodies, such as local user groups and SHGs. Both are DFID partner states. A recent study (Johnson, Deshingkar, and Start 2003) reaches two interesting conclusions.

The first conclusion is that political decentralization in MP has been less effective in addressing the needs of the poor than expected because of "the failure to challenge [the] well-entrenched power of the village chiefs, the *Sarpanches*" (Johnson, Deshingkar, and Start 2003, vi). The government's attempt to challenge the power of these authorities by empowering village councils (*gram sabhas*) and putting power back into the ruling party machinery through District Planning Committees failed. *Gram sabhas* remain controlled by existing leaders, they have not increased political competition, and they are poor in resources and ineffective. In other words, the functioning of formal democratic structures (for example, reserved constituencies of women or low castes) has been substantially undermined by informal power relations.

The second conclusion is that, despite a more limited process of political decentralization in AP (even some hostility to Panchayati raj), the government's populist approach to development (its *janmabhoomi* program of community development through watershed rehabilitation, joint forest management, and women's credit) has empowered the poor in more effective ways. Contributing factors include the AP government's need to secure political support among its key constituencies (women, backward castes, agricultural laborers) especially in face of painful reforms (Johnson, Deshingkar, and Start 2003,11); program delivery arrangements, which brought public officials close to the people even while weakening the *panchayats*; and the creation of incentives for political participation through populist schemes delivered to the poor, which ensured better attendance and participation in AP *gram sabhas*, even though they were bureaucratically controlled (ibid).[7]

The *negative* finding (decentralization empowers local elites to capture resources from the poor) is consistent with a stream of recent research emphasizing that the existence of a strong center that is able and willing to resist the power of local elites (to earmark funds, support strong local staffing, and so on) is a necessary precondition for decentralization (e.g., Tendler 1997).[8] It also speaks to the more general theme that democracy and poverty reduction are not

---

7. The research was undertaken before the ruling of the 2004 elections. The fact that the AP government dramatically lost power suggests, perhaps, the limitations of this political strategy, and the growing unpopularity of the government's reform agenda.

8. The Indian state of West Bengal is often cited as a case that exemplifies effective decentralization based on a strong center providing long-term support.

necessarily mutually supportive. The *positive* finding (populist, central programs can empower) draws attention to the importance of wider political systems and electoral strategies for enhancing the political capabilities of the poor.

Political Representation and Poverty Reduction

In both states, poverty reduction programs and decentralization were shaped by political interests of the government in power, as well as by state-wide caste/class structures (historical continuity of upper caste/class dominance in MP, and historical challenge to landowning dominant castes in AP). But while political strategies worked in favor of the poor in AP, they were less able to do so in MP.

Despite limited political decentralization, the government of Andhra Pradesh put efforts into central anti-poverty programs (such as subsidized rice, credit for women, watershed rehabilitation) that worked for the poor because their interests had become part of the government's electoral strategy; that is to mobilize necessary electoral support from women, low castes, and laborers in face of unpopular reforms. In other words, the wider political system (the nature of political constituencies and party competition) enabled the poor in Andhra Pradesh to develop a political capacity that they did not have in Madhya Pradesh.

Put another way, poor and unorganized people do not have a chance for political representation unless their interests can become a weapon in the struggles of the professional political field (Bourdieu 1991, 188; in Gledhill 1994, 139). The politicization of poverty is necessary for the empowerment of the poor. Making poverty a public, moral, and political issue is often the basis upon which the poor gain leverage by making power work to their advantage through enrolling elite interests, through pro-poor coalitions, and from competition between elite groups (Moore and Putzel 1999). This view of political representation argues against both interest group economism's zero-sum view of structurally opposed interests dividing up the power cake (ibid), and voluntaristic approaches to empowerment through capacity building.

Rights-based approaches to poverty reduction also depend upon effective politicization. Rights awareness and legal aid may be important first steps, but if the rights concerned do not become part of a political agenda, and if those whose rights need to be protected do not comprise a political constituency, the outcomes are unlikely to be very positive. Inter-state *adivasi* (tribal) migrant laborers and construction site workers in India are a case in point since they fail to become a constituency for political parties, line departments, or labor unions, and remain subject to appalling exploitation despite the existence of progressive Indian labor laws (Mosse 2004b).[9]

One difficulty, as Sandra Pepera (2002) notes, may be that "most countries do not define themselves by their poverty, so we cannot assume that poverty reduction is at the heart of politics in developing countries." It is political systems—not policy—that determine the interests and identities that shape the democratic process. Political systems have their own logic, which may or may not enhance the political capabilities of the poor. Since votes are rarely cast simply on the basis of economic interests, the development of political capability among the poor depends upon the adoption and manipulation of identities that allow effective representation. These are often caste, religious, language, or ethnic identities.[10] The problem is that while political systems determine the identities around which people gain empowerment, interests framed in "communal" terms can become self-limiting and dangerous, especially when—as is common—they turn to violence and conflict among the poor themselves.[11]

There is a wider dilemma, often glossed as "political manipulation." Empowerment depends upon political representation, but political capacity

> "POLITICAL SYSTEMS—NOT POLICY—DETERMINE THE INTERESTS AND IDENTITIES THAT SHAPE THE DEMOCRATIC PROCESS. POLITICAL SYSTEMS HAVE THEIR OWN LOGIC, WHICH MAY OR MAY NOT ENHANCE THE POLITICAL CAPABILITIES OF THE POOR."

---

9. Artisanal fishing communities along the Indian coast are another group of the poor who are unable to acquire the political capacity to protect their interests (against mechanized operations) within mainstream politics, largely because current boundaries preclude coastal constituencies.

10. My work in Tamil Nadu shows that even local struggles over resources are increasingly expressed in such terms. When wealthy farmers illegally divert common water sources to their dry land cash crops, poor farmers organize and petition the district authorities as Dalits, alerting the officials to "imminent communal riot." They do so because they understand that this is the language that will secure state backing for local disputes, that will ensure that the next morning four jeeps will arrive in the village with local officials and police to resolve the conflict. Women also use the politics of identity tactically to secure necessary access to resources and services.

11. Growing awareness of this fact may have played its part in the turn against the Hindu nationalist party, the BJP, in India's 2004 national elections.

is gained at the cost of conceding power to a political system with its own logic about maximizing votes, retaining power and coalitions, disseminating ideology, and the like, which further concentrates political capital (Bourdieu 1991, Gledhill 1994). Of course, this does not preclude strategic manipulation by the poor from below. But in India and elsewhere, disillusionment with party politics has fuelled a variety of extra-political social movements with the aim of increasing the capacity of the poor to organize around their interests as forest users, fishermen, indigenous people, and the like. Sometimes these organizations are linked to international NGOs.

Governance, Sector Reform, and Politicization: Contradictions

Moore and Putzel (1999) rightly point out that development agencies need a far greater understanding of the different political systems and scenarios in which they intervene (politically, inevitably), in order to identify opportunities to strengthen the political capabilities of the poor. Developing an operational political analysis is complex and difficult, and it will certainly involve revisiting some existing policy concepts (community-driven development, participation, and social capital, to name just three). The good news, perhaps, is that in the end, effective government—a goal of most donors—is the best condition for developing such political capabilities (ibid). Effective government means, among other things, a center able to defend the interests and rights of the poor; institutionalized populist policies that enable poor people's organizations to access resources or claim rights (including labor rights and land reform); and competition for the votes of the poor through relatively stable party line-ups.[12]

The bad news is that once again, development is most likely to occur where it is already half accomplished (ibid). The poor are rarely well served by weak governments that mobilize their votes in the short term through patronage and violent identity politics. Moreover, the politicization of development programs can often work against the poor. The sectors and schemes that attract most political attention and priority for funding are often those high-profile programs that offer most opportunities to redistribute resources to political supporters so

---

12. The emphasis on governance and stability is crucial, and Chua (2003) offers a timely warning about the dangers of rapid democratization in the context of free-market growth bringing disproportionate wealth to market dominant ethnic minorities.

as to generate political capital cashed as votes. Comparing different types of poverty reduction schemes in India, for example, Farrington (2002) draws a contrast between the National Housing Scheme and the National Old Age Pension Scheme. The former (involving large lump sum payments) is high profile and subject to political interference and corruption, while the latter performs well in terms of poverty-reducing impacts but lacks "political champions" and so is never expanded.

Politicization of this kind acts as a powerful break on reform. The power sector, for instance, is a rich source of election funds. Here, as Sumir Lal points out, political interference is the result of—not the cause of—utilities mismanagement and the "redistribution" of public funds (helped by Indian election funding rules). The problems here are how to depoliticize the power sector, how to contend with internal resistance, and how to rectify the subservient relationship of sector managers to political leadership (Lal 2003). The key point is that poverty reduction is always political, but the way in which interventions are politicized has a significant bearing on the interests of the poor.

Depoliticize or Politicize? Contradictions of Sector Reform

A focus on power relations brings out some contradictions in current policy frameworks, for instance, between the demands of public sector reform (corporatization) and rights-based approaches and good governance (democratization). Sector reform attempts to order public institutions in prescribed terms (autonomous from the political and elected civic bodies). At the same time, striving for democratic rights and entitlements can involve violating these institutional norms (Coelho 2003, citing Partha Chatterjee). Karen Coelho (2003) illustrates the point with a case of urban water supply in Chennai (Madras). Her ethnography shows that the engineers and frontline staff who put public sector reform and corporatization into practice tend to equate the citizenry with private paying consumers. In these terms, slum-dwelling poor people are further marginalized as non-paying, non-deserving, difficult customers (i.e., with few legitimate claims to water rights). On the one hand, the engineers regard group rights-based claims to water and politics more generally as a disorderly nuisance, a rabble; on the other, the poor do not present their claims as individual consumers filling out complaints forms, but collectively, publicly, and confidently in the currency of rights as members of political society.

Donor-Client Power Relations

One final point, which can only be mentioned, is that any poverty reduction strategy that boasts an empowerment component *must* take into account donor-client relations and the political interdependences of donor and country-level coalitions. As the sharp conditionality of 1980s structural adjustment lending is replaced by debt-relief initiatives linked to pro-poor policy reform, PRSPs, Comprehensive Development Frameworks, sector-wide approaches (SWAps) and the like, and as aid relationships are re-framed in the language of partnership or local ownership, these goals need careful conceptual and operational scrutiny.

References

Arun, C. Joe. 2004. "From outcaste to caste: The use of symbols and myths in the construction of identity; A study of conflict between the Paraiyars and the Vanniyars in Tamil Nadu, south India." PhD diss., University of Oxford.

Bailey, F. G. (Frederick George). 1969. *Stratagems and spoils: A social anthropology of politics*. Oxford: Blackwell.

Baumann, Pari. 2000. Sustainable livelihoods and political capital: Arguments and evidence from decentralization and natural resource management in India. ODI Working Paper 136. London: Overseas Development Institute.

Bourdieu, Pierre. 1977. *Outline of a theory of practice*. Cambridge: Cambridge University Press.

———. 1991. *Language and symbolic power*. Ed. John B. Thompson, trans. Gino Raymond and Matthew Adamson. Cambridge: Polity Press.

Cheater, Angela. 1999. Power in the postmodern era. In *The anthropology of power: Empowerment and disempowerment in changing structures*, ed. A. Cheater. London: Routledge.

Chua, Amy. 2003. *World on fire: How exporting free market democracy breeds ethnic hatred and global instability*. London: Arrow Books.

Coelho, Karen. 2003. Unstating "the public": An ethnography of reform in an urban public sector utility in south India. Paper presented at the EIDOS Workshop on Order and Disjuncture: the Organisation of Aid and Development, London.

Dumont, Louis. 1980. *Homo hierarchicus: The caste system and its implications*. Complete revised edition. Chicago: Chicago University Press.

Durlauf, Steven N. 2002. The Empirics of social capital: Some skeptical thoughts.

Roundtable Paper. Washington, DC: World Bank, Social Development Department.

Farrington, John. 2002. Poverty reduction prospects in India: What Difference does state politics make? Presentation for ODI/DESTIN conference, Putting Politics Back into Development: Are We Getting There? London, May 22.

Fiedrich, Marc. 2002. "Domesticating Modernity: Understanding Women's Aspirations in Participatory Literacy Programmes in Uganda." PhD diss., University of Sussex.

Foucault, Michel. 1980. *Power/knowledge: Selected interviews and other writings, 1972-1977*. Ed. Colin Gordon. New York: Pantheon Books.

Gledhill, John. 1994 (2000). *Power and its disguises: Anthropological perspectives on politics.* London: Pluto.

Harriss, John. 2002. Civil society: Universal concept or donor fad? Presentation for ODI/DESTIN conference Putting Politics Back into Development: Are We Getting There? London, May 22.

James, Wendy. 1999. Empowering Ambiguities. In *Anthropology of power: Empowerment and disempowerment in changing structures.* Ed. Angela Cheater. London: Routledge.

Johnson, Craig, Priya Deshingkar, and Daniel Start. 2003. Grounding the state: Poverty, inequality and the politics of governance in India's panchayats. ODI Working Paper 226. London: Overseas Development Institute.

Jenkins, Rob. 2002. Domestic politics and the WTO. Presentation for ODI/DESTIN conference Putting Politics Back into Development: Are We Getting There? London, May 22.

Kumar, Sanjay and Stuart Corbridge. 2002. Programmed to fail? Development projects and the politics of participation. *Journal of Development Studies* 29 (2): 73–103.

Lal, Sumir. 2003. *Political factors affecting power sector reform in India: An internal discussion note.* New Delhi: World Bank.

Leach, E.R (Edmund Ronald). 1964. *Political systems of Highland Burma: A study of Kachin social structure.* Cambridge: Cambridge University Press.

Manor, James. 2002. User committees: A potentially damaging second wave of decentralisation. Draft paper, accessed via www.panchayats.org

Moore, Mick and James Putzel. 1999. Thinking strategically about politics and poverty. IDS Working Paper 101. Brighton: Institute of Development Studies.

Mosse, David. 2002. *Adivasi migrant labour support: A collaborative programme, consultant's report.* Western India Rainfed Farming Project. India: DFID.

———. 2003a. *The rule of water: Statecraft, ecology and collective action in south India.* Delhi: Oxford University Press.

———. 2004a. *Cultivating development: An ethnography of aid policy and practice* London: Pluto.

———. 2004b. On the margins in the city: Adivasi seasonal labour migrants in western India. Paper for Livelihoods at the Margins Conference, SOAS, 8th & 9th July.

Nelson, Nici and Sue Wright. 1994. *Power and participation.* London: Intermediate Technology Publications.

Pepera, Sandra.   2002.   Can PRSPs influence the national politics of poverty reduction? Presentation for ODI/DESTIN conference Putting Politics Back into Development: Are We Getting There? London, May 22.

Sahlins, Marshall. 1999. Two or three things that I know about culture. *Journal of the Royal Anthropological Institute of Great Britain and Ireland* 5 (3): 399–421.

Saxena, N.C.   2001. Issues in panchayats. Draft paper accesses via http://www.panchayats.org.

Scott, James. 1985. *Weapons of the weak: Everyday forms of peasant resistance.* New Haven: Yale University Press.

Tendler, Judith. 1997. *Good government in the tropics.* Baltimore and London: John Hopkins University Press.

Wade, Robert. 1982. The System of administrative and political corruption: Canal irrigation in south India. *Journal of Development Studies* 18 (3): 287–328.

Weber, Max 1964 (1947). *The theory of social and economic organization.* Ed. Talcott Parsons. New York: Free Press of Glencoe; London: Collier-Macmillan.

5. Empowerment and Institutional Change: Mapping "Virtuous Circles" of State-Society Interaction

Jonathan Fox, University of California Santa Cruz

Many of the reasons why pro-poor institutions are needed to encourage poverty reduction were spelled out in the *World Development Report 2000/2001* (World Bank 2000). Many of the institutional logics that explain why some public agencies are more pro-poor than others were detailed in the *World Development Report 2004* (World Bank 2003). However, the causal processes through which institutions *become* pro-poor are less well understood. Purely deductive reasoning is not sufficient. Specifically, how do reform innovations scale up and spread out, moving from enclaves or experiments to influence entire agencies, entire regions, or entire nation-states?[1] The approach sketched here is based on the proposition that pro-poor reform initiatives are likely to have broader and deeper institutional effects if they are accompanied by strategic interactions between policymakers and civil society counterparts that help the latter to identify and overcome obstacles to change.

This paper focuses on the interaction between formal and informal power relations in the process of institutional change, based on an interactive approach to state-society relations (Fox 1992a, 1996). This approach suggests that public institutions whose leadership attempts to move them in more pro-poor directions will have only limited results if they rely solely on their own formal

---

1. For a useful recent intellectual history of related theoretical debates in the fields of political science and public administration, see Olsen (2004).

authority. In practice, institutions operate based on combinations of formal and informal power resources. Formal power resources refer to official mandates, including the administrative, legal, and political authority assigned to carry them out. At the same time, these *de jure* mandates and authority structures are also influenced by *de facto*, informal power relations. While the former may be quite visible, the latter are often deeply embedded and well hidden from outsiders. In other words, official administrative mandates may compete with alternative and often conflicting incentive structures to determine patterns of actual institutional behavior. These contending incentive structures shape the context both for under-performance and for corruption. Both are driven by tension between official and *de facto* incentive structures.

Informal power resources include social capital relationships that exist within and between institutions as well as those that reach across the state-society divide. Informal powers also include *political* capital, which refers to resources that generate the capacity to seek to change the balance of power. Forms of political capital include intra- and extra-institutional credibility, as well as a willingness to use (and create) leverage to influence other actors. Political capital is grounded in a combination of networks of social capital, the capacity to deploy institutional resources, as well as a willingness and capacity to use the media to inform public debates over the issues at stake.[2] Like social capital, the idea of political capital has a certain "you know it when you see it" quality. This certainly limits its measurability, but not its relevance.

The capacity of policy implementers to use both formal and informal powers to divert or to capture pro-change directives from above is well known. The determinants of reformers' capacity to use their powers (both formal and informal) to move from weaker to stronger positions has received less analytical attention (for exceptions, see Houtzager and Moore 2003; Fung and Wright 2003). When both pro-poor policymakers and social actor counterparts start out with limited leverage over state and social actors who oppose institutional

---

2. The effective investment of political capital requires entrepreneurship, especially since it often involves some degree of risk. While it is very common for policymakers to take risks, especially with other people's resources, in practice it is rare for policymakers to take the specific kinds of risks involved in encouraging the empowerment of poor people and the transformation of public institutions into pro-poor actors. Such risks involve accepting the uncertainties inherent in partnering with autonomous poor people's organizations, which by definition bring their own goals and strategies to the table.

change, the result is a chicken-and-egg problem that requires deliberate strategies to crack. In other words, how can pro-poor actors inside and outside institutions break out of a relatively static "low power equilibrium" in which both sets of counterparts lack leverage?

An interactive approach to institutional change suggests that pro-poor reforms require changes in three distinct arenas: within the state itself, within society, and at the state-society interface. Each of these three arenas involves both formal and informal power relations. If one looks at pro-poor institutional change through this lens, one can frame the reform process as one driven by contending cross-sectoral coalitions. In this approach, the reform process depends on changing the balance of power between pro-reform actors embedded in both state and society and anti-reform actors, who are also embedded in state and society. While the anti-reform forces in state and society are very likely to constitute a *de facto* coalition closely linked through informal ties, pro-reform forces do not necessarily coordinate their efforts. Potential pro-reform coalition partners may share objective interests in institutional change, but past experiences may feed mutual wariness and distrust that limit cooperation across the state-society divide.[3] Only unusually entrepreneurial reformists are willing and able to take the political risks involved in reaching out to build pro-reform cross-sectoral coalitions. This process of cross-sectoral coalition-building requires its own set of investment strategies, which involve both social and political capital. Here international donors can play a key role.

To address the chicken-and-egg problem noted above, the challenge is to discover how to trigger and sustain "virtuous circles" of mutual empowerment between institutional reformers and social actors in the public interest.[4] This path-dependent, iterative process can be driven by two interlocking processes. First, reformers within the institutions need to encourage policy environments that tangibly reduce the costs and risks associated with poor people's collective action. Second, poor people's organizations need to scale up, both horizontally and vertically, in order to gain the combination of monitoring capacity and bargaining power necessary to offset the anti-poor elements embedded within the institutions. To maximize the potential for state-society synergy, this process

---

3. On the "rational wariness" of poor people's organizations to engage with participatory policy reforms in less-than-democratic settings, and "intersectoral trust as a resource for reform that requires investment," see Fox and Gershman (2000), and Fox (2003).

4. Putnam's (1993) landmark study put the analysis of such virtuous circles on the agenda.

involves the construction of cross-sectoral coalitions, which in turn both require and generate bridging social capital between institutional and social actors.

To show what this approach means in practice, this paper focuses on the varying degrees to which policy reforms that formally permit participation by organized poor people actually lead to power-sharing in practice. I begin with four conceptual issues: (1) empowerment vs. rights, (2) virtuous circles vs. informal power, (3) economies of scale, and (4) the role of empowered participatory governance. There follows a brief review of the empirical findings of several studies that mapped patterns of regional variation in pro-poor institutional change in rural Mexico. The specific programs studied include the Community Food Councils (DICONSA), the Regional Development Funds (INI), the Municipal Development Funds (SEDESOL) and Rural Development in Marginal Areas (SAGAR). Appendix 1 sketches out the methodological implications of this approach, including the complementary roles of institutional ethnography, the subnational comparative method, and the use of quantitative indicators that aggregate qualitative data. Appendix 2 provides an example of a brief set of related suggestions made to Mexico's Social Development Ministry.

Empowerment vs. Rights

Power is often treated as an implicitly one-way capacity, but it is more usefully understood in terms of relationships.[5] Empowerment involves changes in power relations in three interlocking arenas: within society, within the state, and between state and society. In this context, it is useful to distinguish empowerment, in the sense of actors' capacities, from rights, in the sense of institutionally recognized opportunities. These two good things do not necessarily go together. Institutions may nominally recognize rights that actors, because of imbalances in power relations, are not able to exercise in practice. Conversely, actors may be empowered in the sense of having the experience and capacity to exercise rights, yet they may lack institutionally recognized opportunities to do so. As figure 1 illustrates, rights and empowerment can

---

5. See Lukes (1974, 31). His three-dimensional view of power transcends the limits of the conventional "A has power over B to the extent that A can get B to do something that B would otherwise not do" approach, including the range of capacities to persuade and induce that can lead to disempowered consent. For related classics in political sociology, see also Bachrach and Baratz (1962), and Bachrach and Botwinik (1992).

FIGURE 1. The reciprocal interaction between rights and empowerment

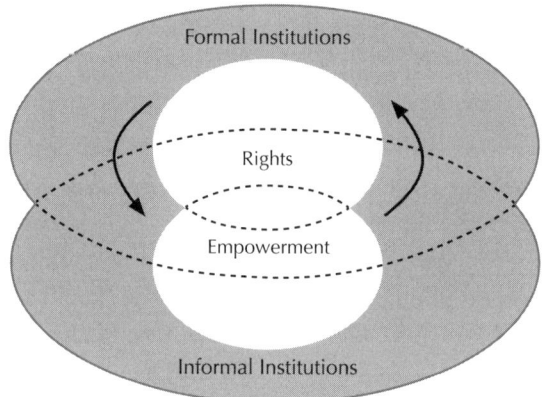

each encourage the other, and indeed they overlap in practice, but they are at the same time analytically distinct.

Virtuous Circles vs. Informal Power

Where pro-empowerment policy initiatives are on the agenda, presumably the state apparatus is not monolithic and at least some elements are more open than others to sharing power with social actors. At the same time, the pre-reform distribution of power is, by definition, unfavorable to those who favor sharing power with socially and economically excluded people. In the case of a study of ten World Bank–funded natural resource management and rural development projects in Mexico and the Philippines, it was the *variation* in commitment to pro-social capital reforms *within* the state apparatus and the Bank that explained the variation in enabling environments for pro-poor empowerment (Fox and Gershman 2000; Fox 2003). The projects that produced the most impressive results, in terms of encouraging actual enabling environments for social capital consolidation, were those that targeted state institutions *already* under the control of pro-participation reformers. By assuming uneven rather than consistent reform implementation, one can also map change across institutions, across geographic space, and over time.

If one accepts the basic assumption of varied rather than uniform policy implementation, then it is not enough to look for associations between the *presence* of a certain set of reforms and social outcomes. A package or menu of pro-empowerment policy reforms is emerging, such as public information access, independent policy monitoring, participatory budgeting, and societal co-management or oversight of social investment and services (Ackerman 2004, Fung and Wright 2003). It is very reasonable to look for the relationships between the presence of such reforms and performance outcomes, but if one looks only at those two sets of indicators, then two problematic assumptions are involved. The first assumption is that the specific reform(s) actually empower social actors in practice, which may or may not be the case.[6] The second implicit assumption is that the appearance of a reform means that it was actually carried out in practice.[7]

Economies of Scale

Official discussions of empowerment are often limited to the most local arenas.[8] For example, the recent *World Development Report*'s generally innovative discussion of the "short route" to accountability is almost exclusively devoted to micro levels of institutional behavior. To the degree that the 2004 *World Development Report* depicts poor people themselves as change agents, they are assumed to be exclusively *local* (families, individuals, implicitly homogeneous communities, or village- and neighborhood-level organizations). While such local arenas are obviously characterized by lopsided state-society power relations,

---

6. For example, information may not be the all-powerful resource that it is often assumed to be. Public access to information without public powers to sanction may turn out to have very limited impact. The literature on transparency has yet to specify with precision the conditions under which it is most likely to generate the effects expected of it—even in the paradigm case of environmental "right to know" laws (e.g., Bui and Mayer 2003). A growing category of transparency reforms is more outward oriented—intended to establish international credibility—than downward oriented, which would make relevant operational and performance information accessible to organized social actors (as in the case of Mexico's PROGRESA program, now known as Oportunidades).

7. For example, if one is interested in understanding under what conditions institutional channels for parent oversight in school management lead to improved performance, then one should look not only at the total number of schools officially involved and the total set of performance outcomes. There is likely to be significant variation across schools in the degree to which they actually share power with parents (rights) and in the degree to which parents are actually able to *exercise* power (empowerment). Methodologically, to find out the degree to which a reform is associated with specific outcomes, one would need indicators of institutional behavior that capture varying degrees of implementation.

8. See, in contrast, Joshi and Moore (2000), and Moore (2001).

they are far from the only, or even necessarily the primary, arena within which the quantity and quality of public service provision are determined.   For example, while rural clinics may lack a supply of subsidized medicines because local officials sell them on the side, it is also possible that they are empty because they were never delivered, having been diverted higher up the chain of authority.   Perhaps basic medicines for poor people were never even budgeted for in the first place.   In other words, even if corruption or underperformance were not issues, sharp social or geographical biases in public spending would remain untouched by the exclusively micro approach of the "short route" to accountability.   Indeed, in this example, to limit the discussion of how to improve institutional accountability to the retail end may be analogous to the "end-of-the-pipe" approach to pollution control.   Without attention paid to source reduction—reduction in the use and emission of toxics—pollution-control efforts are inherently limited and inefficient.   Similarly, unless transparency, accountability, and participatory co-governance poverty-reduction policies *scale up* to address problems throughout the chain of institutional decision making, their impact will be inherently limited.

Scaling up pro-empowerment reforms does not imply the substitution of meso- or national-level institutional measures for local efforts.   A grounded scaling-up process involves bringing together local pro-empowerment actors, allowing them to exchange experiences and see what an agency is doing in the bigger picture, to defend one another from possible reprisals, and to deliberate about which joint strategies are most likely to succeed.   For example, it would be difficult for local pro-empowerment actors to make informed decisions about which policymakers are reliable coalition partners without information about their track records in other regions or in past positions, and other counterpart social actors would be the most credible sources of such information.   The fundamental issue is that the opponents of empowerment—not to mention of accountability—are institutionally embedded throughout the chain of authority.   Their power relies in part on economies of scale.   To *change* the balance of power, pro-empowerment actors also need economies of scale.

Scale provides social actors with more than increased bargaining power; it provides better information as well.   The problems that civil society monitoring is supposed to address are produced by vertically integrated authority structures; therefore, effective monitoring processes require parallel processes of vertical integration as well (Fox 2001). A broad perspective on how the system works can also guide the investment of political capital, helping poor people's organizations target their limited leverage to those pressure points where they are most likely to break bottlenecks. To do this effectively, insider allies are often key. Allied policymakers can sometimes provide some degree of protection from reprisals, which is necessary to allow virtuous circles to unfold. In addition, lack of transparency about formal and informal authorities, as well as the nature

"UNLESS TRANSPARENCY, ACCOUNT-ABILITY, AND PARTICIPATORY CO-GOVERNANCE POVERTY-REDUCTION POLICIES SCALE UP TO ADDRESS PROBLEMS THROUGHOUT THE CHAIN OF INSTITUTIONAL DECISION MAKING, THEIR IMPACT WILL BE INHERENTLY LIMITED."

of their webs of support from non-state actors, means that civil society actors need insider counterparts to provide information that will allow them to focus pro-poor reform pressures where decisions are really made in practice.

The Role of Empowered Participatory Governance

Around the world, a wide range of institutional experiments have been carried out that involve various forms of state-society power-sharing in regard to public sector management and resource allocation.[9] This broad category of initiatives, which includes but is not limited to now well-known experiences such as participatory budgeting and parent co-management of schools, can generate the kind of mutually empowering synergy discussed at the beginning of this chapter. Their dynamics build on, yet are qualitatively distinct from, more conventional and adversarial forms of pluralism, which involve the checks and balances associated with contending organized interests. While participatory governance bodies institutionalize conflict—if successful, bounding it—they also create deliberative mechanisms that can turn what would otherwise be zero-sum confrontations into win-win solutions. The main factor that limits the potential effectiveness of empowered participatory governance is that, in contexts in which the informal distribution of power is highly lopsided, they can be easily co-opted to provide a democratic veneer

---

9. See the notable recent comparative analyses of cases from around the world by Ackerman (2004), and Fung and Wright (2003).

to pre-existing power imbalances (Fung and Wright 2003). These analysts conclude that such experiments are most likely to work when high levels of "countervailing power" are present (a reference to dense, locally grounded representative social actors). This certainly sounds plausible, but the insight is problematic insofar as it implies that the likely scope for such institutional innovations is quite limited, and it does not indicate how countervailing powers can be *bolstered*.[10] The interactive approach sketched above was developed precisely to suggest a more dynamic framework. This is the moment to turn to the empirical discussion of actual institutional experiences with the scaling up of participatory governance institutions in a series of Mexican rural development programs.

Mapping Institutional Change by Analyzing Varied Terms of State-Society Engagement

This section will highlight findings from a series of studies that each mapped variation in informal power relations within a set of rural development programs that all included institutionalized opportunities for Mexican indigenous peoples' organizations to share decision-making power with the public sector. Some of these programs included power-sharing bodies at the community levels; others operated at regional levels and represented dozens of communities, while others created bodies that operated at both levels. All were federal programs of national scope, and all provoked varying degrees of resistance from authoritarian elites embedded in both state and federal government. Most of the field research focused on cross-regional variation within the state of Oaxaca, though some studies also included interstate comparisons. The research was conducted between 1982 and 2000. All of the programs are still in operation, with varying degrees of federal support.

The DICONSA Rural Food Store Network

The Mexican government has long intervened in consumer food markets with a variety of direct and indirect policy instruments, including a gradual and uneven shift from generalized to targeted subsidies (both systems overlapped for an extended period). The first significant targeted rural consumer program

---

10. This issue recalls one of the basic problems with Putnam's (1993) classic study: the circular "them that has, gets" explanation of where social capital comes from. Among other critiques, see Fox (1996).

focused on remote, low-income areas, creating thousands of community-managed local stores that were supplied by the retail distribution branch of the government food company (DICONSA). The stores sold basic foods, and their main impact was to weaken local grain oligopolies, most notably in corn deficit regions. Beginning in 1979, the program pursued its first systematic attempt to use community participation and oversight to encourage public accountability on the part of the food distribution company. The key institutional innovation was to scale up rural consumers' opportunities and capacities for oversight by creating regional councils that would meet regularly at the DICONSA warehouses charged with supplying the rural stores. Each warehouse supplied several dozen stores. This regional level of organized participatory oversight was critical because the warehouses proved to be the key site for possible diversion of subsidized food to private elites. In many of these rural regions, these councils were the first autonomous and representative civil society organization to be tolerated by the government. The local store management committees and the regional councils were launched by the program's national network of grassroots organizers, which was initially independent of the ruling party. Though this outreach network was purged early on after a backlash from regional elites, many of the participatory councils, once launched, continued to function (Fox 1992a).

The distinction between formal and informal power relations becomes clear when one compares the varying degrees of autonomous representation actually achieved by these regional councils. There was a high degree of cross-regional variation in the balance of power between the DICONSA operational apparatus and the regional councils. The patterns of variation depended on the distribution of pro-reform actors within the agency on the one hand, and on the varying degrees of community control over the local stores within each warehouse's regional supply area on the other. Where neither were present, there was little participation or accountability. At the other extreme, where both were present, major breakthroughs were made. Where pro-reform actors from above did not find counterparts from below, and vice versa, progress was limited and stalemate often ensued (Fox 1992a).

By the mid-1980s, approximately one-third of the councils had achieved some degree of autonomous oversight capacity, and national networking efforts have ebbed and flowed since then. Many food distribution councils spun off separately or reinforced autonomous regional producer associations. In spite of the highly targeted nature of the program, it has long lacked high-level policy support. Nevertheless, the rural store network survived several finance ministry attempts to liquidate it during the late 1990s, and it continues to operate more than 22,000 outlets.[11]

INI's Indigenous Development Funds

Starting in 1989, the Mexican government dramatically increased the economic development role of its National Indigenous Institute (INI) as part of the National Solidarity Program. Inspired largely by the DICONSA food council experience, the INI created dozens of regional economic development councils. Elected representatives of indigenous producer organizations jointly evaluated grassroots funding proposals, and co-signed the checks together with INI outreach officials. These councils achieved widely varying degrees of autonomy and capacity, and in some regions INI operational officials managed to exclude autonomous organizations. Table 1 compares the INI's own ranking of varying degrees of pluralist consolidation of these regional councils with an independent assessment based on a survey of local civil society leaders. The variable of pluralist practices is key because in political systems characterized by persistent authoritarian clientelism—all other things being equal—"participatory" councils will be controlled by pliant official membership organizations that lack the autonomy necessary to represent their members.[12] As in the case of the rural food store program, economic and political support from federal level pro-empowerment policymakers made pluralism and autonomy possible in a significant minority of the regional councils, and the program continues to exist.

---

11. See www.diconsa.gob.mx. For a recent government-sponsored evaluation, see GEA (2003). No recent independent scholarly or NGO evaluations exist.

12. *Clientelism* refers to imbalanced bargaining relationships in which political loyalty is exchanged for material benefits. The term is widely used to refer to an unduly open-ended set of relationships, and its usage often overlaps heavily with the more general category of political bargaining and inducements. For example, "pork barrel politics," the process through which legislators seek to channel material benefits to their districts, is simply politics at work, and could even be construed as a form of accountability to constituents. The qualified term *authoritarian* clientelism is distinctive because it refers to exchanges of loyalty for benefits that are backed up by actual or potential threats of coercion. Carrots that are backed up by sticks are a special kind of carrot. For further discussion, see Fox (1994b).

TABLE 1. Degrees of consolidation: INI ranking and independent confirmation

Leadership council	INI 1991 budget (M $million) implicit ranking	Independent confirmation of INI ranking[1]	Pluralistic[2]
Jamiltepec	1,700	Yes	Yes*
Miahuatlán	1,700	Yes	Yes*
Guichicovi	1,350	Yes	Yes*
San Mateo	1,300	No (too high)	0
Cuicatlán	1,250	Yes	Yes
Tlacolula	1,250	Yes	Yes*
Guelatao	1,200	Yes	Yes*
Juquila	1,200	No (too high)	0
Nochixtlan	1,200	No (too high)	0
Huamelula	1,100	No (too high)	0
Tuxtepec	1,000	Yes	No*
Huautla	800	No (very low)	Yes*
Laollaga	800	No (too low)	Yes*
Copala	700	Yes	No*
Ecatepec	700	No (too high)	No
Silacayoapan	650	Yes	?
Temascal	600	Yes	Yes*
Lombardo	600	Yes	Yes*
Ayutla	500	Yes	Yes*
Tlaxiaco	500	Yes	Yes*

Source: Fox 1994a.

[1] Independent confirmation means that there was a good fit between INI's implicit leadership council ranking and the results of a survey of twelve Oaxaca-based grassroots development experts (as of March 1992).

[2] "Yes" means that the representative, autonomous organizations in the region had some access to the leadership council. "No" means that significant groups were excluded or seriously underrepresented. "0" means that there were virtually no strong representative producer organizations reported in the region, and the fund was INI-run. Asterisks (*) indicate the presence in the region of groups in the autonomous Coordinadora Estatal de Productores de Café de Oaxaca (CEPCO) network.

The Municipal Development Funds

The Mexican government's Social Development Ministry launched its first large-scale investment program for rural municipal investment funds at the beginning of the 1990s, also as part of the National Solidarity Program. The program has continued to grow since then, with substantial support from the World Bank and the Inter-American Development Bank. This program lacked regional power-sharing bodies, but local investment decisions were supposed to be made by grassroots communities (and not just by local governments, which administered the funds). To a large degree, this worked in those communities that already exercised a high degree of assembly-style decision making. A study of a representative cross-section of Oaxacan municipalities found that in a clear majority of cases, project selection decisions were made by the community assembly rather than by the mayor, a local subgroup, or external actors, as indicated in figure 2. This experience was not generalized, however. The key pro-participation variables in Oaxaca—dense horizontal social capital and autonomous submunicipal village governments—were not widespread in other low-income rural states; therefore, the rural municipal funds probably empowered authoritarian municipal governments elsewhere, most notably in

FIGURE 2. Key project-selection decision makers

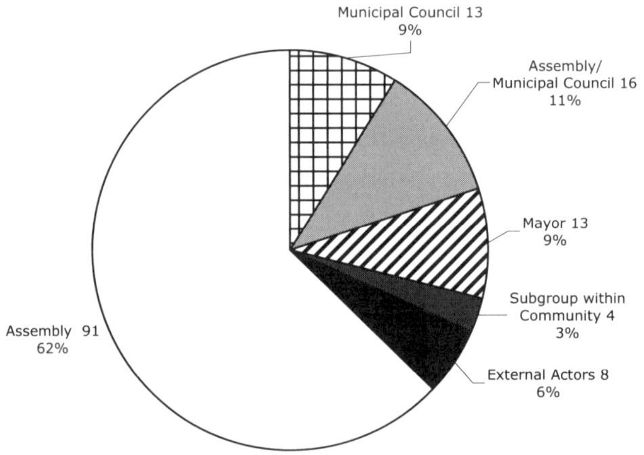

Source: Fox and Aranda 1996.

Chiapas and to some degree in Guerrero (Fox 1997, 1999, 2002).[13] In contrast to the DICONSA and INI programs, this one lacked both a local capacity-building component and regional participatory councils that could become counterweights. The participatory elements of the program lacked strategic support from federal reformists, leaving its fate up to local and state political dynamics.

Rural Development in Marginal Areas Program

In the late 1990s, the Agriculture Ministry, with World Bank funding, launched another rural investment program in low-income areas. Informed in part by the INI program experience, regional councils of elected representatives of producer organizations were established with a mandate to choose among grassroots funding proposals. In contrast to the INI program, however, the Agriculture Ministry's decentralization process created more formal and informal opportunities for state government officials to influence or veto council decisions. Most state government officials involved, even in the relatively pluralistic state of Oaxaca, opposed power-sharing with producer organizations. As a result, few regional councils gained autonomy or capacity. Most of those councils that did were broken up or starved for funds. The program was also launched in the three-state Huastecas region, with similar exclusionary results, as summarized in figure 3.

Comparative Analysis of Transparency and Participation Provisions

The results in terms of actual power-sharing were uneven in all cases, but the degree of exclusion varied significantly. Differences include both varied degrees and scales of transparency and participation measures (see table 2), as well as varied informal relationships between state and societal actors.[14] On the society side, one of the key variables was the capacity and willingness of social organizations to engage with the opportunities for participation. On the state side, the key variables included whether regional representative bodies existed, as well as their degree of oversight and decision-making capacity. In all cases the

---

13. This variation in local power relations is clearly widespread; therefore, the default assumption should be variation rather than community-level homogeneity. See, for example, Williams et al. (2003).

14. Table 2 also includes a reference to the more recent PROGRESA/Oportunidades transfer payment program, for contrast. For a brief discussion, see the policy note addressed to the Mexican Social Development Ministry, appendix 2.

FIGURE 3. Degrees of inclusion of autonomous indigenous producer organizations in regional councils

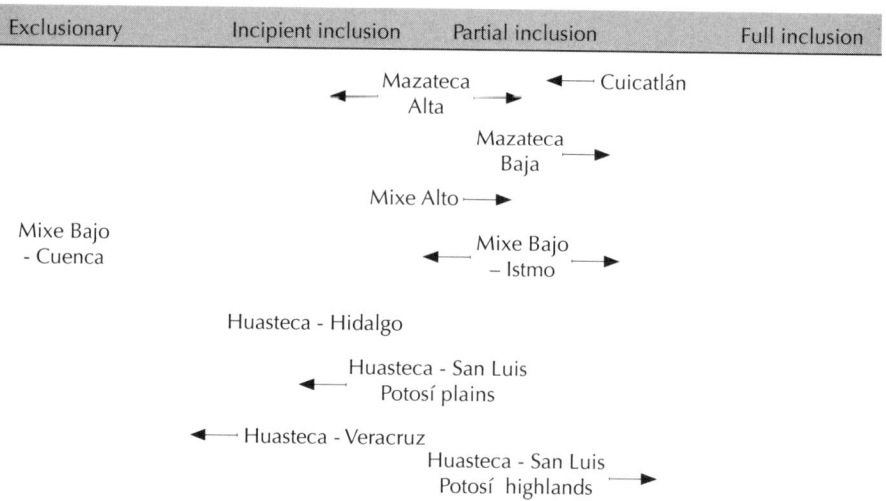

Source: Fox 2003.

Note: Arrows indicate whether councils are moving toward more or less pluralism, or whether they are being pulled in both directions at once. The assessments are based on field interviews as of August 1999.

TABLE 2. Comparison of formal power-sharing opportunities across Mexican rural anti-poverty programs

	Community organization with co-governance role	Regional level collective representation for social organizations	Consistent provisions to make program decisions and operations transparent to beneficiaries	Formal autonomy from state governments (all are federal programs)
Regional Food Councils (DICONSA)	Yes	Yes	Yes	Yes
Regional Funds (INI)	Partial	Yes	No	Yes
Municipal Funds (SEDESOL)	Yes	No	No	No
Regional Councils (SAGAR)	Partial	Yes	No	No
PROGRESA (Oportunidades)	No	No	No	Yes

degree of power sharing generated in practice depended heavily on the presence of a *de facto* faction within the implementing agency, at both the top and middle levels, that was willing to take the risks inherent in partnering with autonomous social organizations.

The dynamics that drive the varying empowerment outcomes in the case of all four rural development programs can be described as a "sandwich strategy" (figure 4). This involves three-way interaction between regional grassroots rural social actors, pro-reform policymakers with actual influence over implementing

FIGURE 4. Sandwich strategy

With pressure from both above and below, the sandwich strategy creates political space and shifts the balance of power between authoritarian elites and movements for rural democratization.

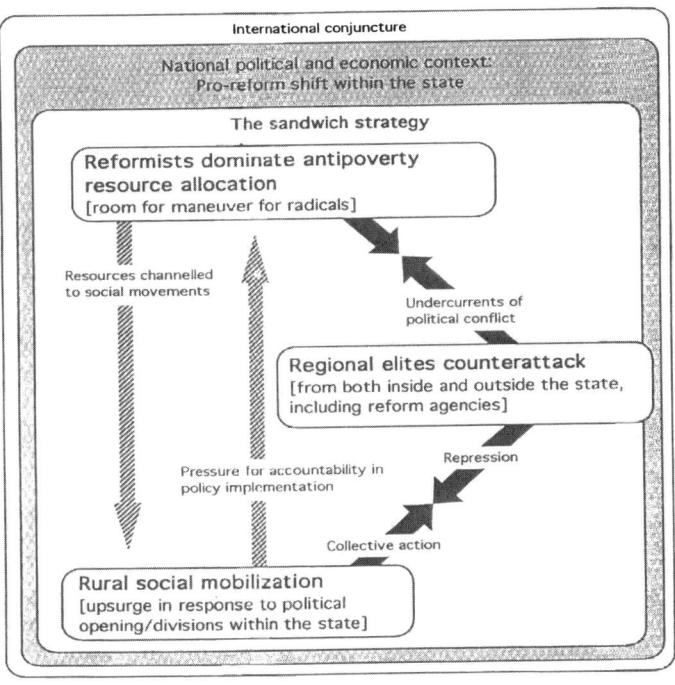

Possible outcome: Increased government accountability in contested policy arena, spreading to other issues.

Probably outcome: Increased peasant capacity to articulate interests.

Source: Fox 1992a.

agencies, and anti-reform regional elites embedded in both the state and society. With pressure from both above and below, the sandwich strategy creates political space and shifts the balance of power between authoritarian elites and movements for rural democratization. A possible outcome is increased government accountability in contested policy arenas, which will spread to other issues. The probable outcome—as autonomous, representative organizations consolidate—is the peasants' increased capacity to articulate their interests.

Concluding Propositions

- Pro-empowerment institutional reforms are driven by mutually reinforcing cross-sectoral coalitions between state and society, grounded in mutually perceived shared interests.
- Institutional reforms that appear to be enabling may not be. They need to be unpacked in terms of their actual coverage, depth, and empowerment effects.
- Pro-empowerment enabling environments require a synergistic package of policy reforms. Transparency, accountability, and participation reforms need each other and are mutually reinforcing.
- Power sharing involves conflict; successful power sharing involves conflict-resolution mechanisms that can be made more successful through deliberative power-sharing institutions.
- Pro-reform cross-sectoral coalitions in favor of empowerment require pro-poor policymakers to invest their political capital in order to give potential civil society counterparts clear signals, tangible incentives to engage, and some protection from backlash.
- To encourage an enabling policy environment for empowerment, support reformers with track records—and support them while they are in their current institutions.

References

Ackerman, John. 2004. Co-governance for accountability: Beyond "exit" and "voice." *World Development* 32 (3): 447–463.

Bachrach, Peter, and Morton Baratz. 1962. The two faces of power. *American Political Science Review* 56 (4): 947–952.

Bachrach, Peter and Aryeh Botwinik. 1992. *Power and empowerment.* Philadelphia:

Temple University Press.

Bui, Linda T. M., and Christopher Mayer. 2003. Regulation and capitalization of environmental amenities: Evidence from the toxic release inventory in Massachusetts. *Review of Economics and Statistics* 85 (3): 693–708.

Evans, Peter, ed. 1996. Government action, social capital and development: Reviewing the evidence on synergy. *World Development* 24 (6): 1119–1132.

Fox, Jonathan. 1992a. *The politics of food in Mexico: State power and social mobilization.* Ithaca, NY: Cornell University Press.

———. 1992b. Democratic rural development: Leadership accountability in regional peasant organizations. *Development and Change* 23 (2): 1–36.

———. 1994a. Targeting the Poorest: The role of the National Indigenous Institute in Mexico's National Solidarity Program. In *Transforming state-society relations in mexico: The national solidarity strategy.* Eds. Wayne Cornelius, Ann Craig, and Jonathan Fox. La Jolla, CA: University of California, San Diego, Center for U.S.-Mexican Studies.

———. 1994b. The difficult transition from clientelism to citizenship: Lessons from Mexico. *World Politics* 46 (2): 151–184.

———. 1996. How does civil society thicken? The political construction of social capital in rural Mexico. *World Development* 24 (6): 1089–1104.

———. 1997. The World Bank and social capital: Contesting the concept in practice. *Journal of International Development* 9 (7): 963–972.

———. 1999. The inter-dependence between citizen participation and institutional accountability: Lessons from Mexico's rural municipal funds. In *Thinking out loud: Innovative case studies on participation instruments,* ed. Katherine Bain. Washington, DC: World Bank.

———. 2001. Vertically integrated policy monitoring: A tool for civil society policy advocacy. *Nonprofit and Voluntary Sector Quarterly* 30 (3): 616–627.

———. 2002. La relación recíproca entre la participación ciudadana y la rendición de cuentas: La experiencia de los fondos municipales en el México rural. *Política y Gobierno* 9 (1): 95–133.

———. 2003. De la teoría a la práctica del capital social: El Banco Mundial en el campo mexicano. *Foro Internacional* 43 (2): 347–405.

Fox, Jonathan, and Josefina Aranda. 1996. *Decentralization and rural development in Mexico: Community participation in Oaxaca's Municipal Funds Program.* La Jolla, CA: University of California, San Diego, Center for US-Mexican Studies.

Fox, Jonathan, and John Gershman. 2000. The World Bank and social capital: Lessons from ten rural development projects in Mexico and the Philippines. *Policy Sciences* 33 (3&4): 399–419.

Fung, Archon, and Erik Olin Wright, eds. 2003. *Deepening democracy: Institutional innovations in empowered participatory governance.* London: Verso.

GEA. 2003. *Evaluación externa del programa de abasto rural operado por DICONSA: Reporte final.* Mexico City: Grupo de Economistas y Asociados.

Houtzager, Peter, and Mick Moore. 2003. *Changing paths: International development and the new politics of inclusion.* Ann Arbor: University of Michigan.

Joshi, Anuradha, and Mick Moore. 2000. Enabling environments: Do anti-poverty programmes mobilise the poor? *Journal of Development Studies* 37 (1): 25–56.

Lukes, Stephen. 1974. *Power: A radical view.* London: Macmillan.

Moore, Mick. 2001. Empowerment at Last? *Journal of International Development* 13: 321–9.

Olsen, Johan P. 2004. The 2003 John Gaus lecture: Citizens, public administration and the search for theoretical foundations. *Political Science and Politics* 37 (1): 69–79.

Putnam, Robert. 1993. *Making democracy work: Civic traditions in modern Italy.* Princeton, NJ: Princeton University.

Snyder, Richard. 2001. Scaling down: The subnational comparative method. *Studies in Comparative International Development* 36 (1): 93–110.

Williams, Glyn, Rene Veron, Stuart Corbridge, and Manoj Srivastava. 2003. Participation and power: Poor people's engagement with India's employment assurance scheme. *Development and Change* 34 (1): 163–192.

World Bank. 2000. *World Development Report 2000/2001: Attacking Poverty.* New York: Oxford University Press.

———. 2003. *World Development Report 2004: Making Services Work for Poor People.* Washington, DC: World Bank.

Appendix 1: Three Methodological Implications

Because of the frequently opaque interaction between formal and informal power relations, conventional methodologies are often poorly equipped to measure the processes of pro-poor institutional change. In this context, it is crucial to transcend conventional dichotomies between small-N qualitative case studies and large-N statistical analyses of easily quantifiable indicators. All the studies reviewed above involved some combination of three mutually reinforcing methodological strategies: the subnational comparative method, institutional ethnographies grounded in political economy, and the aggregation of qualitative indicators of institutional behavior.

The Relevance of the Subnational Comparative Method

The spread of decentralization has increased interest in the subnational comparative method. Its relevance is not limited to the comparison of distinct subnational governments, however. It can also be applied to nominally national programs that in practice experience significant regional variation. Within the field of comparative politics, some analysts have long noted the risks of "whole-nation bias" in comparative studies that rely on national averages which in turn mask sharp variation. A focus on subnational variation allows for comparisons that control for social, political, and economic differences, which in turn allow analysts to focus on relationships between specific institutional changes and social actors. This approach also allows one to increase the number of observations, and thereby address the classic problem of "many variables, small N" (Synder 2001).

Institutional Ethnography

Much of the analysis of institutions is based on deductive assumptions about their internal logics. However, frameworks that impute internal logics based on visible internal and external incentive structures do not necessarily lend themselves to explaining the variation inherent in pro-poor institutional change. Without a full understanding of the "actually existing" internal logics of specific institutions, it is difficult to specify accurate indicators of how they change, especially when formal indicators of change may hide informal patterns of continuity. The ethnographic study of the actual operations of an institution, informed by a political economy framework, is often needed to identify bottlenecks with precision. Such an approach is just as valid for analyzing social actors as it is for public institutions.[15] This approach can inform the design both of effective strategies for changing the institution's internal incentive structure and of performance indicators that will actually indicate what they are supposed to indicate.

Aggregate Qualitative Indicators of Institutional Behavior

There is an emerging package of policy reforms associated with enabling institutional environments for transparency, accountability, and social participation. To measure progress and identify bottlenecks, reform-specific indicators are needed to measure the inherently uneven degree to which they are actually carried out. These implementation processes can be seen as intervening variables between the more easily quantified economic investment inputs and social indicator outputs.

Reform-specific indicators need to measure two distinct dimensions of institutional change. One involves its extension, the degree to which reforms are actually implemented throughout a given public agency, or agencies. The other dimension involves the depth, or intensity, of reforms: indicators are needed to capture the difference between "lite" reforms and those with greater leverage or impact. A clear example of this range of variation would be the World Bank's official spectrum of pro-participation reforms, including information dissemination, consultation, shared deliberations, power sharing, and actual devolution of decision making to social actors.

Indicators of transparency reform implementation might include measures of the quality, reliability, quantity, practical accessibility, and social relevance of the information disclosed. Accountability indicators might include both attempts at and outcomes of enforcement efforts. Indicators of social participation might address its scope, autonomy, ethnic/gender/class composition, scale, and impact. Clearly, most of these indicators are not easily *quantified*, but that does not mean that they cannot be *measured*, using qualitative benchmarks. The proposition here is that institutional ethnography can ground qualitative assessments that can in turn be aggregated to produce generalizable results, revealing patterns of variation that would not otherwise be apparent.

---

15. For an example of the application of this approach to the study of internal democracy within a regional peasant organization, with a focus on internal checks and balances, see Fox (1992b).

Appendix 2: Policy Note to Mexican Social Development Ministry & World Bank Mexico Department, July, 2003

This policy note will focus on the institutions of *inclusion*, rather than on the processes of exclusion. I will focus on research issues regarding the dynamics of exclusion/inclusion specifically in terms of existing social programs. My point of departure is that analysis of institutional behavior requires the tools of institutional analysis.

I would like to make two broad points. The first one is about the coverage of and access to social programs, and the second is about the lessons of institutional innovations and the policy experience until now. First, how do we develop a more reliable and comprehensive field-based sense of how the institutional mechanisms of coverage of and access to social programs *actually work in practice*? This process has both a macro dimension and a micro dimension.

The macro dimension involves figuring out, with a bit more precision, what fraction of the total target population is actually reached by a particular program, and perhaps how that coverage has changed over time. For example, among SEDESOL programs, a contrast between the relative coverage of Oportunidades, DICONSA-rural, the urban tortilla program, and the Jornaleros Agrícolas program would be useful here. The first two have very broad coverage, while the second two cover only a small subset of the eligible populations (the tortilla program used to have a fully national coverage of the low-income urban population, until its number of beneficiaries was reduced by approximately 90 percent during 2001-02). The descriptive question about program coverage is a first step toward getting a better frame on the analytical question of *why* programs vary so much in terms of relative coverage, as well as toward facilitating future discussion about which programs should expand their coverage and which ones should not.

The micro dimension of analyzing how social programs reach people involves developing field-based assessments of how people access these programs in practice. This is necessary to find out what the barriers are, as experienced by potential beneficiaries. These barriers are not always obvious at a distance from the access point. For example, how difficult is it to register a change of address? This may seem like a minor point, but problems with this *trámite* (administrative step) alone could end up removing large numbers of eligible people from the rolls.

Second, there is now a widespread consensus among public policy analysts regarding the value of transparency, accountability, and citizen participation in terms of creating incentives for improved institutional performance and service delivery. There is also significant evidence of the synergy between these three institutional reform processes, with transparency encouraging both participation and accountability, and accountability further encouraging more participation, in a process of virtuous circles, or positive feedback loops. In brief, institutional reforms that promote transparency and accountability create an enabling environment for participation, which in turn broadens the constituency of stakeholders that support more transparency and accountability.

This is fine at the conceptual level, but several major puzzles remain. For example, empirically, there is limited information about the degree to which these enabling reforms are actually implemented and accessible to citizens in practice.

If we look at transparency initiatives, based on past research I would hypothesize that, in order for transparency to have its intended positive effects, investments in the production of information require quality control and targeting to ensure that the information provided is the kind that is relevant and useful to encourage constructive collective action, especially by the principal stakeholders: actual or potential program beneficiaries. In addition, investments are needed to increase the capacity of these information consumers to access and use it effectively. In short, supply-side transparency strategies are necessary but not sufficient.

Similarly, accountability reforms that appear plausible in theory or on paper may or may not work in practice, and field research on how they actually work in practice is needed. For example, many of the reforms involving the creation of offices of *controloría social,* though very positive, are limited by the fact that they focus primarily on fighting corruption, and some tend to be very Internet-driven, which is of limited relevance to most program beneficiaries. A narrow focus on corruption does not address the broader issue of using accountability mechanisms to improve institutional performance more generally. It would be useful to consider the creation of publicly accessible ombudsman offices—agencies with clearly established autonomy from the interested parties responsible for agency performance.

In terms of the need for more research on how public participation can contribute to the performance of social programs, the fact that it is difficult to measure participation with precision does not mean that it cannot be analyzed. To begin with, one can look at existing programs in terms of whether they have any *instancias de participación* (participatory forums) at all, whether such bodies are institutionalized, whether they have actual decision-making powers or are merely consultative, and whether they are scaled up or strictly local and therefore have less leverage over public institutions. Some government programs have many years of experience with scaled-up, decision-making kinds of state-citizen power-sharing bodies, as in the case of the DICONSA-rural *Consejos Comunitarios de Abasto* and the INI's *Fondos Regionales*. Research on these institutional innovations would benefit from a combination of qualitative/institutional and quantitative methods.

More generally, among the array of institutional reform options, which ones make the most difference? The answer is not obvious. What factors promote the most consistent implementation of those enabling policies that do work? I suggest that a comparative approach to these questions would be very useful, both across programs and across regions and localities.

To sum up this second point, I would like to make one general proposal, followed by an additional observation. The general proposal is that it would be useful to assess, across a range of social programs, the degree and nature of the **actually functioning institutional mechanisms of transparency, participation, and accountability**. The example of Oportunidades having a recourse mechanism on paper that may have been rarely exercised in practice would be an important test case.

The additional observation involves the open question of unintended inter-institutional inter-active effects. My understanding is that the research on basic education and health services in Mexico finds both very broad coverage and very uneven quality, which raises the issue of how accountability mechanisms can work better to raise the lower end. There may be aspects of Oportunidades operations that are relevant and interactive. Specifically, I propose the following hypothesis to be tested in the field, based so far on limited ethnographic evidence: There may be **cross-institutional disincentives** for Oportunidades program beneficiaries to push for accountability in their education and health services, since it would potentially put their status in Oportunidades at risk. For example, if parents complain about teacher or doctor absences, or about ineffective teaching or health services, then those teachers or doctors could drop those families from the list of beneficiaries. To my knowledge, there is no mechanism to prevent this from happening, since in practice there is little effective recourse once one is dropped from the list. If such cross-institutional disincentives for accountability *do* exist, then that suggests the need to rethink and propose new and more effective accountability mechanisms.

In conclusion, we still do not know very much about how good practices and potentially enabling environments for institutional change actually spread from limited enclaves of innovation to transform entire institutions.

6. Measuring Empowerment: Country Indicators

Jeremy Holland and Simon Brook, Centre for Development Studies, University of Wales Swansea

The *World Development Report 2000/2001* (World Bank 2000) proposes a poverty reduction strategy based on promoting opportunity, facilitating empowerment, and enhancing security. The report recognizes the critical role empowerment plays in reducing poverty. The integration of empowerment in poverty analysis is hindered, however, by the difficulty of measuring and monitoring progress towards empowerment (Grootaert 2003). Unless empowerment is measured, it is impossible to draw useful conclusions regarding the relationship or correlation between empowerment levels and poverty reduction, or the outcomes of strategies designed to empower individuals and groups (Strandberg 2002). This paper identifies and justifies a selection of indicators for measuring empowerment.

The measurement of empowerment is hindered by three factors: multiple definitions, the intangible and non-material nature of empowerment as bound up in institutions (sets of rules) and processes (the operation of those rules), and the contextual nature of those institutions and processes. Clearly, measurement of progress towards empowerment at the country level requires a definition that is standardizable, and a set of indicators that are observable, objective, and measurable. Only with these tools can we generate information that is comparable across populations and over time.

Among the current activities of the World Bank's Empowerment Team is a five-country Measuring Empowerment (ME) study. The output of that work will include intervention-level indicators and instruments for measuring empowerment. The purpose of this paper is specifically to identify a set of country indicators that measure changes in empowerment and to associate those indicators with changes in the poverty status of different groups within countries. The approach requires three elements: (1) data which can be gathered through existing household and other surveys and data sources (but which may require additional analysis to that normally undertaken); (2) intermediate and direct indicators derived from existing survey instruments; and (3) indicators (both intermediate and direct) which are not yet captured by existing data collection instruments.

Below we briefly review the conceptualization and definition of empowerment employed by the ME study and then identify a set of indicators against that framework to measure empowerment.

Conceptualizing and Defining Empowerment: The Study Framework

In the background papers to the ME study, the team defines empowerment as increasing the capacity of individuals or groups to make choices and to transform those into desired actions and outcomes. The form of individual empowerment ranges from passive access to institutions through active participation to influence and finally control. (The Empowerment Team's analytic framework is found on page 120.)

The study framework posits that the extent to which actors are empowered depends on both their asset base (agency) and the institutional context (opportunity structure) in which they operate. Assets include skills, information, education, organizational capacity, psychological resources (such as self-confidence), and financial and material resources. The institutional context refers to the existence and operation of formal and informal rules, including laws, regulations, norms, and customs, that determine whether individuals have access to different assets and whether they can use the assets to achieve desired outcomes.[1] In analyzing the relationship between people's

---

1. For the purposes of the study, institutions are viewed to comprise four sets of rules: (1) allocation rules, which determine the distribution of goods or services; (2) inclusion rules, which define who can engage in what; (3) accountability rules, which determine responsibility and authority; and (4) procedural rules, which determine the sequencing of roles and responsibilities.

assets and institutional structure, it is necessary to consider the influence of personal attributes, such as gender, ethnicity, age, religious identity, and political affiliation.

The relationship between agency and opportunity structure is played out in different contexts or domains. The framework distinguishes three domains—state, market, and society—in which the individual is a social actor, an economic actor, and citizen, respectively. Each domain has its own set of subdomains. There is no prior assumption that empowerment in one domain relates to empowerment in another, although overlaps are of course possible. Each domain therefore needs to be considered separately.

Within the analytical framework, these domains provide the context for the iteration of agency and institutions at different levels of proximity—national, intermediary, and local. The institutional basis for empowerment is increasingly proximate to the individual as one moves from national to local. It is important to note here that the ME study analytically recognizes differences between levels of empowerment. Even if individuals or communities gain resources at the local level, for example, this does not necessarily mean that they will be empowered at the intermediary or national level (Moore 2001; Fox 1996).[2]

Towards Indicators for Measuring Empowerment

The ME study conceptual framework sets up an iterative relationship between these three concepts of agency, opportunity structure, and empowerment. The elements, separated for data collection purposes, are pulled together in the analytical stage of the research. In translating the analytical framework into a measurement tool, the study makes a distinction between intermediate and direct indicators of empowerment. We discuss these briefly below.

As country-level methodologies develop, these categories will be re-examined and re-defined or expanded. According to Ruth Alsop, this review will need to make a clearer distinction between accountability and responsiveness. This conceptualization recognizes the contribution of Freire (1973), Sen (1985; 1992), Fals Borda (1988), Kabeer (1992; 1996), Bennet (2003), Smulovitz et al. (2003), and others who emphasize the institutional nature of power and powerlessness. It further fits with the *Empowerment Sourcebook* (Narayan 2002) statement that powerlessness is embedded in the nature of institutional relations so that an institutional definition of empowerment should be used in the context of poverty reduction.

2. Witness rural communities in Mexico that are "institutionally thick" and yet remain powerless and poverty stricken. Politically empowering change often requires a spatial scaling up of social networks and networking (Fox 1996).

Intermediate Indicators of Empowerment

Intermediate indicators—those that mediate final empowerment outcomes—measure either agency (determined by asset base) or opportunity structure (measured by formal or informal institutions). The relationship between agency, opportunity structure, and empowerment as conceptualized does not try to predetermine the direction of causality between these elements. Hence, we are not predicting that empowerment will neatly fit into a cause and effect relationship with enhanced agency or institutional transformation. Instead, we recognize that this relationship will be country-context specific.

Agency

The ME study defines an individual's agency in terms of his or her asset base and appears on first glance to be biased towards the agency of individuals rather than on the agency of groups. This is largely the effect of the study's data collection method, which uses the household survey as its main instrument. The study recognizes, however, the importance of collective action and organizational effectiveness. Empowerment releases individual capabilities but also challenges (geographical or social) communal silence (Freire 1973) by amplifying collective voice.

When comparing measures of agency with indicators and analysis of institutional change (below), it is important to identify which forms of collective action have the highest impact in terms of challenging and progressively influencing institutions and processes.

Many measures for intermediate indicators of empowerment are already generated by Living Standards Measurement Survey (LSMS)-type survey instruments. Table 1 summarizes some of the asset data that could be generated through existing instruments. The table identifies which existing instruments gather information on these indicators so that the module proposed in this paper can use questions drawn from these instruments.[3] Before comparing these differences to empowerment outcomes and institutional change, data will need to be disaggregated by gender and other social variables to probe social differences in asset ownership.

---

3. Consequently, if the proposed module is implemented as part of an LSMS or an Integrated Questionnaire for the Measurement of Social Capital, then some questions will not be necessary.

Table 1. Intermediate Indicators of Empowerment: Agency (available from existing survey instruments)

Asset base	Indicator	Existing sources/instruments
Psychological assets	Self-perceived exclusion from community activities	IQMSC – section 5
	Level of interaction/sociability with people from different social groups	IQMSC – section 5
	Capacity to envisage change, to aspire	IQMSC – section 6
Informational assets	Journey time to nearest working post office	IQMSC – section 4
	Journey time to nearest working telephone	IQMSC – section 4
	Frequency of radio listening	IQMSC – section 4
	Frequency of television watching	IQMSC – section 4
	Frequency of newspaper reading	IQMSC – section 4
	Passable road access to house (periods of time)	IQMSC – section 4
	Perceived changes in access to information	IQMSC – section 4
	Completed education level	SCAT Household Questionnaire section 2
Organizational assets	Membership of organizations	IQMSC – section 1
	Effectiveness of group leadership	IQMSC – section 1
	Influence in selection of group leaders	IQMSC – section 1
	Level of diversity of group membership	IQMSC – section 1
Material assets	Land ownership	LSMS – economic activities module
	Tool ownership	LSMS – economic activities module
	Ownership of durable goods	LSMS – economic activities module
	Type of housing	SCAT Household Questionnaire – section 2
Financial assets	Employment history	LSMS – economic activities module
	Level of indebtedness	LSMS – economic activities module
	Sources of credit	LSMS – economic activities module
	Household expenses	LSMS – housing module
	Food expenditure	LSMS – food expenditures module
	Occupation	SCAT Household Questionnaire – section 2
Human assets	Literacy levels	LSMS – education module
	Numeracy levels	LSMS – education module
	Health status	LSMS – health module

Note: IQMSC = Integrated Questionnaire for the Measurement of Social Capital; LSMS = Living Standards Measurement Survey; SCAT= Social Capital Assessment Tool.

Some of the indicators in table 1 can be investigated within two or more asset categories. For instance, access to communications infrastructure can be investigated within the informational assets category or the material assets category. Where this is the case, they have been placed in just one category in the table. Where duplication of sources occurs, only one source is suggested in the table.

"THE CHALLENGE OF MEASURING INSTITUTIONS IS FURTHER COMPLICATED BY THE HUGE GAP THAT EXISTS BETWEEN THE PRESENCE OF SETS OF RULES AND THE MESSY, POLITICIZED, AND SOCIALLY CONSTRUCTED REALITY OF THE ENACTMENT OF THOSE RULES."

Opportunity Structure
In the ME study conceptual framework, opportunity structure comprises rules and their enactment that determine access to assets and the use of those assets. Table 2 summarizes the institutions (presence of rules) and processes (enactment of rules) that can be measured in the range of domains and subdomains mapped in the ME study.[4]

The measurement of opportunity structure, with its focus on the rules that govern social relations, is not easily captured by household survey instruments. The challenge of measuring institutions is further complicated by the huge gap that exists between the presence of sets of rules and the messy, politicized, and socially constructed reality of the enactment of those rules. Measurement of institutions will therefore require a mixed method approach that includes national-level tracking of legislation, regulation, and procedure (table 2 "Presence of Rules") and local in-depth probing of the operation of formal and informal institutions (table 2 "Enactment of Rules").

Where possible, local in-depth analysis should be participatory to enable local stakeholders to map, measure, and analyze their institutions, thus opening up the possibility of empowerment through institutional transformation.[5] Participatory analysis can be further stimulated by combining participatory

---

4. We argue here that rules tend to be formally adopted but can be enacted through both formal and informal institutional contexts. The enactment of rules in informal contexts is bound up in societal norms, beliefs, customs, and values (Kabeer 2000, 22).

5. Examples of this type of process include local monitoring of service delivery (for example, police station procedure or health delivery) through partnerships of service providers and users.

M&E effectively with rights-awareness building and capacity strengthening for different social groups, including service providers.

Direct Indicators of Empowerment

Direct indicators of empowerment relate to the four forms of empowerment identified by the ME study: passive access, active participation, influence, and control. We adopt the study's analytical framework table to map in table 3 an indicative list of empowerment indicators that might be elicited using a household survey module.[6] These indicators measure empowerment in the following three areas:

1) Opportunity to use influence/exercise choice;
2) Using influence/exercising choice; and
3) Effectiveness of using influence/exercising choice in terms of the desired outcome.

These data are not available currently through any other survey instrument and will need to be gathered through a new module. We have restricted the scope of indicators to those that are objectively measurable or at least which allow for a scoring of qualitative assessment against a common scale. It is worth noting that some measures for these indicators will be less reliable (in terms of respondent consistency), particularly those that indicate sensitive aspects of institutional power relations within households and communities.

---

6. An important element in the design of the LSMS questionnaire is that it can be changed quickly and easily, either in response to the field test or over the years as policy needs change.

Table 2. Intermediate Indicators of Empowerment: Opportunity Structure

(Where no number is given indicating an existing data source, then the data is not readily available in existing sources. Where an index is given, i.e. Civil Society Index, an indication of important areas included in the index is given in italics.)

Domain: State
Sub-domain: Justice

Presence of rules (institutions)

Formal

- Number of international instruments and conventions on civil and political rights ratified (6)
- Index of Civil Liberties (1) *(independent judiciary; civil and criminal rule of law)*
- Press Freedom Index (1) *(legislation protecting press freedom)*
- Civil Society Index (3) *(civil and criminal rule of law)*
- Number of laws/acts providing protection from political oppression
- Number of laws/acts providing protection from social oppression
- Number of laws/acts providing protection from domestic violence
- Number of anti-corruption laws/acts (2, 4)
- Number of statutory rights conferred by a national framework of criminal, commercial and international law

Enactment of rules (processes)

Formal

- Number of reported incidents of government interference in police force per year
- Corruption Perception Index (5) *(transparency/ accountability/ freedom from corruption to ensure accessible justice with respect to public officials and professional groups (including investment in capacity building and in HR education/ training)*
- Number of corruption cases tried per year
- Number of constitutional courts and national legal mechanisms protecting national constitutional rights (for example, to fair trial, protection from torture and detention without trial, divorce rights) (8)
- Number of affordable and accessible public redress procedures (for example, independent HR commissions, ombudsmen and complaints tribunals)
- Number of cases tried in the national formal legal system enforcing statutory rights per year
- Number of cases tried in local formal legal systems (through local government enacting by-laws) enforcing statutory rights per year
- Annual public expenditure in rights awareness campaigns
- Number of extra-judicial killings per year (8)
- Number of extra-judicial disappearances per year (7, 8)

Informal (Cultural)

- Number of human rights violations occurring as a result of the enforcement of customary rights through structures of customary authority per year (8)
- Number of crimes rooted in living, customary or religious law (e.g. honor killing, domestic violence and sexual abuse) reported per year (8)
- Number of women using local informal justice/ dispute resolution systems per year
- Number of ethnic / religious minority groups using local informal justice / dispute resolution systems per year
- Number of complaints regarding accessibility and equitability of local informal justice / dispute resolution systems per year

Existing data sources/indices

   (1) Freedom House
   (2) Political Risk Services: International Country Risk Guide – Political Risk Rating
   (3) CIVICUS
   (4) World Bank Governance Datasets
   (5) Transparency International
   (6) Office of the UN High Commissioner for Human Rights
   (7) UN Working Group on Enforced or Involuntary Disappearances
   (8) US State Department – Country Reports on Human Rights Practices

Domain: State
Sub-domain: Politics

Presence of rules (institutions)

Formal

- Number of international instruments and conventions on civil and political rights (including the right to participate) ratified (3)
- Index of Political Rights (1) *(constitutional support for free, fair and regular elections; accountability of monarchy)*
- Index of Civil Liberties (1) *(freedom of association and political organization)*
- Civil Society Index (2) *(freedom of association and political organization)*
- Number of laws/acts protecting freedom of association and political organization (4)
- Number of formal rules of inclusion/ exclusion in political life (for example, India: formal rules for % inclusion)

Enactment of rules (processes)

Formal

- Index of Political Rights (1) *(fair electoral process; elected representatives endowed with real power; effective opposition parties; freedom of association enforced)*
- Civil Society Index (2) *(freedom of expression enforced)*
- Index of Civil Liberties (1) *(freedom of expression enforced)*
- Number of cases alleging discrimination filed per year
- Number of cases alleging discrimination won per year

Informal (cultural)

- Number of people influenced by tribal / religious leaders in their voting choice per election
- Number of reported cases of local elites using informal hierarchical power relationships as form of social control per year
- Number of women participating in political processes per year
- Number of people from ethnic / religious minorities participating in political processes per year
- Number of women in positions of political influence per year
- Number of people from ethnic / religious minorities in positions of political influence
- Number of reported cases of local feudal or patron-client power relations per year
- Number of private armed groups operating per year

Existing data sources/indices

   (1) Freedom House
   (2) CIVICUS
   (3) Office of the UN High Commissioner for Human Rights
   (4) US State Department – Country Reports on Human Rights Practices

Domain: State
Sub-domain: Service Delivery

Presence of rules (institutions)

Formal

- Number of laws/acts ensuring freedom of information (1)
- Number of international instruments and conventions on Economic, Social and Cultural (ESC) rights (including the right to education and to highest attainable standard of physical and mental health) ratified (2)
- Percentage of nominal annual budget allocation in line with PRS priorities (4)
- Number of formal initiatives supporting free access to information on service entitlements per year (1)
- Number of formal initiatives supporting free access to information on government service delivery performance (1)

Enactment of rules (processes)

Formal

- Number of national data systems accessible to the public as percentage of total number of data systems
- Percentage of real annual budget allocation in line with PRS priorities (for example, government expenditure on health and education as percentage of GDP) (4)
- Number of public consultations on policy proposals/ formulation per year
- Number of women attending public consultations on policy proposals/ formulation per year
- Number of inclusive platforms for participation in service delivery
- Number of formal legal actions upholding ESC rights with respect to government conduct per year
- Number of reported cases of corruption amongst "street level" bureaucrats per year
- Corruption Perception Index (3) *(transparency/ accountability/freedom from corruption amongst "street level" bureaucrats, public officials and professional groups, including investment in capacity building)*
- Percentage of total population unable to access at least one basic service in the previous year due to cost (4)
- Percentage of total population unable to access at least one basic service due to physical distance (4)
- Percentage of total population unable to access at least one basic service due to social distance (4)

Informal (cultural)

- Number of complaints regarding transparency and equity of operation of informal social transfer systems (for example, *Zakat*) per year
- Percentage of women able to access public service entitlements during previous year
- Percentage of total ethnic/ religious minority population able to access public service entitlements during previous year

Existing data sources/indices

- (1) Privacy International – Country Reports
- (2) Office of the UN High Commissioner for Human Rights
- (3) Transparency International
- (4) World Bank Country Policy and Institutional Assessment

Domain: Market
Sub-domain: Credit

Presence of rules (institutions)

Formal

- Number of laws/ Acts supporting pro-poor credit rules
- Existence of regulatory framework for credit and savings provision

Enactment of rules (processes)
- Number of formal transparency and accountability mechanisms and procedures for credit provision agencies
- Number of reported cases of corrupt practices within credit provision agencies per year as percentage of total transactions

Informal (cultural)
- Percentage of informal credit sources providing credit with exploitative terms and conditions
- Percentage of women accessing formal credit sources per year
- Percentage of women accessing informal credit sources per year
- Percentage of ethnic/religious minorities accessing informal credit sources per year
- Percentage of ethnic/religious minorities accessing formal credit sources per year
- Percentage of women controlling use of credit within household

Domain: Market
Sub-domain: Labor

Presence of rules (institutions)
Formal
- Number of international instruments and conventions on Core Labor Standards, the rights of the child and the right to work (full employment, choice and conditions of work) ratified (1, 2, 3)
- Number of laws/acts supporting pro-poor labor shifts in labor market segmentation
- Number of regulatory reforms for economic participation over preceding two years
- Legislation exists to ensure equal remuneration for men and women
- Legislation exists to ensure non-discrimination in respect of employment and occupation
- Legislation exists to ensure protection of children and adolescents
- Legislation exists to abolish forced labor (3, 4)
- Legislation exists protecting the right to organize and bargain collectively (4)
- Core labor standards are implemented through regulatory frameworks (3)
- Institutional framework exists for government – employer – trade union partnerships

Enactment of rules (processes)
Formal
- Total number of cases filed against employers for non-compliance with core labor standards per year
- Number of cases filed by the state against employers for non-compliance with core labor standards per year
- Percentage of employers complying fully with state regulations as percentage of total number of employers

Informal (cultural)
- Percentage of women able to choose their employment options
- Percentage of ethnic/religious minorities able to choose their employment options
- Percentage of people from identified caste able to choose their employment options
- Percentage of households with no rigidly defined and inflexible roles for household members
- Percentage of households with equal workloads for adult members
- Percentage of total workforce working as bonded labor (4)
- Percentage of school-age children working to contribute to household income (4)

Existing data sources/indices
- (1) International Labour Organisation
- (2) Office of the UN High Commissioner for Human Rights
- (3) World Bank Country Policy and Institutional Assessment
- (4) US State Department – Country Reports on Human Rights Practices

Domain: Market
Sub-domain: Goods
(production/consumption, including basic needs)

Presence of rules (institutions)

Formal
- Number of international instruments and conventions on ESC rights, including land rights, standard of living, freedom from hunger and social security ratified (1)
- Pro-redistribution legislation for access to and control over productive assets (including land) (2)
- Regulatory framework in place for market based allocation of basic needs and goods
- Pro-transparent and simple regulation exists for small businesses (2)
- Legislation exists ensuring fair trading conditions/ relationships between buyers and sellers (2)

Enactment of rules (processes)

Formal
- Number of formal social policy commitments to basic needs provision backed by budget execution (2)
- Percentage of threatened evictions prevented through formal legal processes and protection (2)
- Percentage of productive assets owned by poorest 20 percent of households
- Percentage of productive assets owned by richest 20 percent of households
- Number of cases of fair-trading violations filed through the justice system per year (2)
- Number of mechanisms for ensuring transparency and accountability amongst product producers and distributors
- Number of complaints regarding transparency and accountability by product producers and distributors per year

Informal (cultural)
- Percentage of women able to inherit property
- Percentage of men able to inherit property
- Percentage of "lower" castes or classes owning property
- Percentage of women within household owning property and productive assets
- Percentage of men within household owning property and productive assets
- Percentage of households with joint ownership of property and productive assets

Existing data sources/indices
  (1) Office of the UN High Commissioner for Human Rights
  (2) World Bank Country Policy and Institutional Assessment

Domain: Society
Sub-domain: Household and Kinship Groups

Presence of rules (institutions)

Formal
- Ratification of Convention on the Rights of the Child (and Convention on Elimination of all Forms of Discrimination Against Women (1, 2)
- Number of legislative responses to the Convention on the Rights of the Child and Convention on Elimination of all Forms of Discrimination Against Women (1, 2)

Formal
- Number of cases filed in the formal justice system enforcing child rights legislation per year (3)
- Number of formal justice cases filed against violators of women's rights legislation per year (2, 3)

Enactment of rules (processes)

Informal (cultural)
- Percentage of cases in which rules governing duties and entitlements relating to accumulation and redistribution within households and kinship groups diverge from joint utility maximizing rules

- Number of women working in occupations socially defined as male occupations as percentage of total women working
- Percentage of women able to travel alone outside of community in the previous year
- Percentage of men able to travel alone outside of community in the previous year
- Percentage of females accessing formal institutions in the previous year
- Percentage of males accessing formal institutions in the previous year
- Number of community advocacy and awareness campaigns against domestic violence and sexual abuse in the previous year

Existing data sources/indices
(1) Office of the UN High Commissioner for Human Rights
(2) World Bank Country Policy and Institutional Assessment
(3) US State Department – Country Reports on Human Rights Practices

Domain: Society
Sub-domain: Community

Presence of rules (institutions)
Formal
- Number of laws/ Acts supporting community level organization and association
- Number of decision-making processes decentralized to local authority control
- Percentage of budget allocation decentralized to local authority control
- Institutional framework exists for local government – civil society – private sector partnerships
- Number of laws/ Acts addressing social, ethnic and religious discrimination

Enactment of rules (processes)
Formal
- Number of public meetings at which the implications of rules are discussed per year
- Percentage of cases in which rules of community membership groups reflect normative formal rules

Informal (cultural)
- Percentage of labor force employed outside any traditionally expected roles based on social identity
- Variance between membership diversity (gender/ social/ ethnic/ religious) of community associations and diversity of local community
- Number of reported cases of community association membership restrictions based on gender/ social/ ethnic/ religious identity per year
- Percentage of decision-making positions with occupied by people from lower castes or classes

Table 3. Direct Indicators of Empowerment

(Numbers in parentheses indicate relevant survey module questions.)

Domain: State
Sub-domain: Justice

Empowerment Indicator

National
- Number of court cases and the time between submission and conclusion of cases
- Percent of positions in justice system per social/ ethnic/ religious group
- Number of national newspapers/ media organizations independent of government influence or control

Intermediary
- Number of local court cases and the time between submission and conclusion of cases
- Percent of positions in local justice system per social/ ethnic/ religious group

Local
- Percent awareness of listed (formal/informal) justice systems (4.1)
- Number of times justice systems used (4.2-4.3)
- Score of effectiveness of justice systems (4.4)
- Score of fairness of justice systems (4.5-4.6)
- Score of gender equity in treatment by justice systems (4.7)
- Score of equity by other stated social variable in treatment by justice systems (4.8)
- Score of accessibility of justice systems (4.9)
- Score of ability to complain about justice systems' performance (4.10-4.11)
- Score of level of independence of police force (4.12)
- Score of confidence in corrupt people facing justice (4.13)

Domain: State
Sub-domain: Politics

Empowerment Indicator

National
- Household survey questions 4.14-4.32 also apply at the national level
- Percent of elected representatives in national government per social/ ethnic/ religious group
- Number of people actively voting in national elections compared to those entitled to vote
- Number of representative and democratic national political parties
- Diversity of representative and democratic national political parties
- Number of national newspapers/ media organizations independent of government influence or control
- Diversity of newspaper/media ownership

Intermediary
- Household survey questions 4.14-4.32 also apply at the regional level

Local
- Percent awareness of local electoral process (4.14)
- Percent interest in local electoral process (4.15)
- Percent entitled to vote in local elections (4.16)
- Percent voting in last local elections (4.17)
- Percent wanting to vote in last local elections (4.18)
- Percent control over their voting choice (4.19)
- Frequency of, and impact of, discussion about local election candidates (4.20-4.23)
- Score of involvement in the local political process (4.24)
- Score of aspiration to be more or less involved in the local political process (4.25)

- Score of number of representatives of national political parties in the local area (4.26)
- Score of degree of influence of elected representative at local level (4.27)
- Score of fairness of local electoral process (4.28)
- Frequency of dissatisfaction with local elected representative (4.29)
- Availability of accountability mechanisms (4.30)
- Frequency of use of accountability mechanisms (4.31)
- Score of effectiveness of accountability mechanisms (4.32)

Domain: State
Sub-domain: Service Delivery

Empowerment Indicator
National
- Score of satisfaction with national executive administration (key line ministries)
- Score of effectiveness of regional executive administration (key line ministries) compared with other social groups

Intermediary
- Score of satisfaction with regional executive administration
- Score of effectiveness of regional executive administration compared with other social groups

Local
- Number of publicly provided services available locally (4.33)
- Percent able to access public services (4.34; 4.37)
- Number of public services used (4.35)
- Score of quality of public services used (4.36)
- Percent individuals that have complained about public service delivery (4.38)
- Percent of households that have complained about public service delivery (4.39)
- Frequency of complaints (4.40)
- Score of satisfaction with outcome of complaint (4.41)
- Score of equitability in addressing needs and concerns (4.42)
- Score of influence of social characteristics on the authorities treatment of people (4.43)

Domain: Market
Sub-domain: Credit

Empowerment Indicator
National
- Score of civil society advocacy activity for pro-poor credit provision
- Percent of credit provision by formal institutions according to social/ethnic/religious group
- Diversity of national credit providing institutions

Intermediary
- Score of consultation levels by credit providing agencies with clients
- Number of partnerships in credit system design and delivery
- Diversity of local formal credit sources
- Diversity of local informal credit sources

Local
- Percent needing to borrow money or goods in past year (4.44)
- Percent borrowing money or goods in past year (4.45)
- Score of awareness of formal/ informal credit services (4.46)
- Score of accessibility to formal credit-providing institutions (4.47-4.50)
- Score of control over loans and savings (4.51-4.52)

Domain: Market
Sub-domain: Labor

Empowerment Indicator

National
- Diversity of national labor organizations
- Percent changes in labor market composition per year
- Score of civil society advocacy activity for labor protection legislation
- Percent presence in capital intensive/ high skill positions per social/ ethnic/ religious group
- Percent difference in salary levels by ethnic/ social/ religious group
- Number of industrial disputes resolved equitably per year

Intermediary
- Score of effectiveness of local labor organizations
- Diversity of local labor organizations
- Number of collective bargaining mechanisms/processes over wage rates/ employment conditions

Local
- Score of control over employment/occupation choices (4.53-4.55, 3.41-3.42)
- Percent involved in household work (4.56)
- Score of time used for unpaid household work and child care (4.57-4.58)
- Score of division of labor and roles within household (4.59)

Domain: Market
Sub-domain: Goods
(production/consumption, including basic needs)

Empowerment Indicator

National
- Score of civil society advocacy activity for redistribution of productive assets
- Score of civil society advocacy activity for basic needs provision
- Percent awareness of national market prices and conditions
- Score of civil society and state advocacy activity for equitable access to markets
- Percent change in national asset ownership per social/ ethnic/ religious group per year
- Percent change in control over national assets per social/ ethnic/ religious group per year

Intermediary
- Score of civil society advocacy activity for (decentralized) basic needs provision
- Number of local buyers of products
- Number of local suppliers of products
- Number of producer cooperatives

Local
- Score of perceived risk/threat of eviction (4.60)
- Score of protection from eviction (4.61)
- Score of influence of social characteristics on asset ownership/access (4.62-4.63)
- Score of gender influence on inheritance rights (4.64-4.66)

Domain: Society
Sub-domain: Household

Empowerment Indicator

National

- Score of civil society advocacy activity for legislation addressing informal patriarchal rules

Intermediary

- Score of community advocacy activity addressing informal patriarchal rules
- Score of civil society monitoring activity of unequal household relations

Local

- Score for distribution of household decision-making power (4.67)
- Score of individual's decision making autonomy (4.68)
- Score of control over one's body (4.69)
- Score of individual mobility (4.70)
- Score of individual access to basic services (4.71-4.72)
- Score of comparative household expenditure on healthcare per individual household member (4.73-4.74)

Domain: Society
Sub-domain: Community

Empowerment Indicator

National

- Number of national networks/ alliances of community organizations
- Diversity of community based organizations

Intermediary

- Score of inter-community networking activity
- Score of authority over local policy process
- Score of authority over local budgets
- Percent of local government budget allocated per social/ ethnic/ religious group
- Score of mobility of social/ ethnic/ religious groups outside their immediate locality

Local

- Percent awareness of main local public service decision makers (4.75)
- Score of involvement in community decision making processes (4.76)
- Score of aspiration to be more or less involved in community decision making processes (4.77)
- Score of influence in community decision making processes (4.78)

References

Alsop, Ruth, N. Heinsohn, and A. Somma. February 2004. *Measuring empowerment: An analytic framework*. Washington, DC: World Bank.

Beall, J. 1997. Social capital in waste—A solid investment? *Journal of International Development* 9 (7): 951–961.

Bennett, L. 2003. *Empowerment and social inclusion: A social development perspective on the cultural and institutional foundations of poverty reduction*. Washington, DC: The World Bank.

Black, J. K. 1999. *Development in theory and practice: paradigms and paradoxes*, 2nd Edition. Boulder: Westview Press.

Fals, Borda O. 1988. *Knowledge and people's power*. New Delhi: Indian Social Institute.

Fox, Jonathan. 1996. How does civil society thicken? The political construction of social capital in Rural Mexico. *World Development* 24 (6): 1089–1103.

Freire, P. 1973. *Pedagogy of the oppressed*. London: Penguin Books.

Grootaert, C. 2003. Assessing empowerment in the ECA region. Paper presented at the Measuring Empowerment: Cross-Disciplinary Perspectives workshop. Washington, DC: World Bank.

Kabeer, N. 2000. *The power to choose: Bangladeshi women and labour market decisions in London and Dhaka*. London: Verso.

———. 1996. Agency, well-being and inequality: Reflections on the gender dimensions of poverty. *IDS Bulletin* 27 (1): 11-21.

———. 1992. Triple roles, gender roles, social relations: The political sub-text of gender training. Discussion paper 313. Brighton, UK: Institute of Development Studies.

Moore, Mick. 2001. Empowerment at last? *Journal of International Development* 13: 321–9.

Narayan, Deepa, ed. 2002. *Empowerment and poverty reduction: A sourcebook*. Washington, DC: World Bank.

Sen, Amartya. 1985. *Commodities and capabilities*. Amsterdam: Elsevier.

——— 1992. *Inequality reconsidered*. Cambridge, Mass: Harvard University Press.

Smulovitz, C., M. Walton, and Patti Petesch. 2003. Notes on evaluating empowerment. Washington, DC: The World Bank.

Strandberg, N. 2002. Conceptualising empowerment as a transformative strategy for poverty eradication and the implications for measuring progress. Available at: www.un.org/womenwatch/daw/csw/empower/documents/Strandberg-EP6.pdf.

World Bank. 2000. *World development report 2000/2001: Attacking poverty*. New York: Oxford University Press.

7. Empowerment at the Local Level: Issues, Responses, Assessments

Michael Woolcock, World Bank and Harvard University

In recent years, the theme of empowerment has assumed an increasingly high profile in international development debates. This paper seeks to address three key issues that advocates and critics of empowerment must confront if the debates are to move forward in constructive ways—which is to say, on the basis of evidence derived from meaningful dialogue, which in turn gives rise to supportable and implementable recommendations. The standard fault lines for such debates are, of course, driven by deeper underlying philosophical commitments, methodological preferences, and disciplinary provincialisms, which characteristically conspire against a common ontological and epistemological basis for initiating and sustaining dialogue and reaching agreement. In debates concerning empowerment within development organizations, an immediate manifestation of this problem is that otherwise reasonable imperatives for indicators to measure empowerment (or to assess the efficacy of policies and projects invoked in its name) quickly descend into, and become a microcosm of, an unsatisfying battle between fundamentally different starting points. Moreover, precisely because these types of differences are largely non-empirical, more and better "evidence" is unlikely to resolve them. Like other such differences (for example, between those representing different religious communities or political parties), identifying and sustaining a basis for respectful dialogue and debate offers the best way forward.

I argue that the search for empowerment indicators is reasonable primarily because it helps all sides in these debates clarify and substantiate the causal nature of the claims they are making, whether being supportive or critical of the broader category of issues encapsulated by empowerment terminology. If we knew what the key indicators of empowerment were (in a general, universal sense), the development community would probably have identified them a long time ago. The fact that we do not have them—or have them in a form that is at best partial and highly imperfect—should be neither a source of embarrassment nor an excuse for ignoring the issue. However, we do have general indicators of development outcomes (health, income, education, and so on) that scholars, practitioners, and policymakers have broadly agreed upon, and with that a subsequent recognition that certain groups—within, but especially between, countries—fare especially badly with respect to those indicators. How and why certain groups persistently achieve such poor outcomes is the right and proper opening question; the empirical and policy challenge is to identify the ways and means by which the processes leading to these outcomes are created and sustained, a good portion of which is likely to amount to something we could call exclusion, and for which the appropriate response at least in part is likely to have something to do with empowerment. If we have gone through such an analysis, a second challenge is then to identify an appropriate set of policy and project responses. A third challenge is then to demonstrate the efficacy of those responses (net of other contributing factors, and vis-à-vis other possible policy responses). This paper seeks to explore each of these three stages in further detail.

Stage 1

Who is excluded from what? Does it matter (instrumentally or intrinsically)? How and why is their exclusion created and sustained?

In many respects, the rhetorical battle to acknowledge that certain groups are consistently and persistently excluded from the development process has been won (for example, World Bank 2000, Narayan 2002), but the war to bring a greater sense of conceptual and empirical rigor to these debates is far from over. This is so partly because the issue in general is intrinsically complex, and partly because the truly difficult questions surrounding process issues—that is, understanding the mechanisms and processes by which certain groups and countries become and remain excluded—require data in forms that do not fit easily with the usual imperatives of large organizations.[1] As such, policy research on empowerment is likely destined for constant controversy, from which it must seek to neither escape (retreating in frustration or fear) nor capitulate (for example, produce numbers that meet short-term demands but at greater longer-term cost).

In my view, the way forward should be one characterized by a two-fold commitment: first, to expand and improve existing household sources on development outcomes and their determinants, which will help us better identify who is excluded from what (and what the aggregate instrumental consequences are); second, to engage in more context- and issue-specific research using mixed methods in order to more accurately determine how and why certain groups start and stay excluded (Tilly 1998), which will help us generate useable data on *process* issues for incorporation into country- or provincial-specific policy responses. The research should use mixed methods because most process issues are best understood qualitatively (though access to panel data would also be desirable); many of the impacts of exclusion concern people's identity and personhood, which cannot adequately be addressed quantitatively (or at least by quantitative methods alone); and it is desirable to test the broader applicability of key emergent themes across larger samples using survey data.

An example of efforts to collect data on empowerment and exclusion comes from an ongoing study in Indonesia on understanding and responding to local conflict (Barron et al. 2004). Like many developing countries, Indonesia has a great variety of ethnic groups, and with them many different customary legal traditions for addressing everyday conflicts, such as those over land, inheritance, petty theft, and domestic disputes. In an era of expanding economic integration and political decentralization, these communities are coming into increasing contact with one another, and as such are confronting issues that are of a scale, frequency, and level of complexity beyond that which their customary laws were ever intended to address. The formal legal system, moreover, may offer

---

1. It is important to keep in mind that intra-country differences on virtually all standard development outcomes are orders of magnitude smaller than those between countries. The wealthiest 20 percent of Pakistanis suffer levels of infant mortality, for example, that are far larger than the poorest 20 percent of the residents of any OECD country (see Pritchett 2003). The policy levers for correcting intra-country differences may be more tangible, but the *really* big differences in welfare remain those between countries.

the long-term possibility of a more universal rule of law, but in the short-term becomes yet another actor competing for legitimacy in matters pertaining to dispute resolution. Villagers thus find themselves negotiating between different rules systems, with a given problem plausibly falling into multiple jurisdictions, and all the attendant problems of adjudication and enforcement capacity that that entails.

What does legal empowerment look like in such contexts? The answer turns in large part on first finding out which groups have the hardest time gaining access to, and a fair hearing from, the court systems, and identifying which groups have to negotiate their way between the largest number of dispute resolution alternatives. In both cases, the groups in question are poor, rural, and minority ethnic communities. A crucial second step is explaining the variation in the degree to which different groups faced with common problems manage to craft enduring solutions. The most effective policy responses initiated to help such communities more effectively address their local level disputes are likely to be ones that complement these strategies. The empirical foundation for understanding and responding to legal empowerment, in short, requires integrated forms of qualitative and quantitative data.

What is true for legal empowerment is true more broadly: if empowerment issues are to be mainstreamed in development, then the empirical basis for doing so needs to be one that is built on a comprehensive and coherent data collection effort that draws on rigorous quantitative and qualitative methods and data. Such efforts should be primarily linked to helping improve basic service delivery for excluded groups in specific country contexts, rather than set up as a separate or parallel activity or agenda.

Stage 2
If disempowerment is indeed the problem, are the corresponding policy/project responses technically sound, politically supportable, and administratively implementable?

Accurate diagnosis is part of the empowerment challenge, but so too must be the crafting of viable, useable responses. Too often those professionally committed to an empowerment agenda frame their policy responses in excessively abstract terms, failing to recognize that such articulations are far too easy to dismiss or—worse—to ignore. Being clear about what they are *against* (for example, human rights violations, an exclusively economic understanding of welfare) rather than *for* is another unfortunate characteristic. Having a firm empirical base on which to infer such responses (as discussed above) is the first step toward improvement; a second is framing the responses in ways that demonstrate their conceptual value-added relative to rival alternatives and are clear about who exactly will carry the recommendations forward, and how.

This task entails being confident about the theoretical principles that underpin both the empowerment proposals and their alternatives, having an informed sense of the capacity of any implementing agency (public, private, or civic), and the likelihood that the proposal will also be able to attract a support base large enough to withstand political and other forms of resistance. If these three conditions are not met, it is unlikely an agenda or policy launched in the name of empowerment will succeed. Put another way, a response to exclusion and disempowerment that is not technically sound (that is, meets high discipline-determined standards), politically supportable (commands endorsement by a sufficiently broad base), and administratively implementable (maps onto a coherent combination of willing and able people and organizational structures) is not a response, and at worst can become part of the problem.[2]

Stage 3

How do we know whether and how these responses are working, and, if so, that they are better than other plausible alternatives?

The final challenge—assuming that some form of response is in fact implemented—is to document whether and how this response achieved its intentions. Evaluations of any kind are difficult to do for a number of good and not-so-good reasons (Pritchett 2002), but are especially difficult when both the issue to be overcome (exclusion) and the means typically employed to redress it (some variant on participation) are deeply enmeshed in social processes.[3]

---

2. This is the sense in which some have argued that pro-poor polices can become poor policies. At least in democracies, securing the support of the middle classes is vital for establishing a coalition large enough to withstand the likely resistance of influential elites.

3. This is another reason for employing mixed methods when doing evaluations of empowerment projects and policies. On the specific challenges posed by social development projects to rigorous evaluation protocols, and some possible responses, see Whiteside, Woolcock, and Briggs (2004).

Moreover, given that certain influential voices in development see little need to focus on responses that are specifically geared towards empowerment—insisting, for example, that economic growth is the best approach to empowering the poor—it would be instructive to know the precise value of empowerment-specific responses, where it lies, and how it can be improved.

> "THE DEVELOPMENT COMMUNITY NEEDS TO RECOGNIZE THAT BY VIRTUE OF BEING IN THE POVERTY REDUCTION BUSINESS IT IS ALSO, NECESSARILY, IN THE REVOLUTIONS BUSINESS."

Thinking about how to design and implement a rigorous evaluation strategy needs to be a central part of all development policies and projects, but especially those implemented in the name of overcoming exclusion or empowering the poor. The development community has too few examples of demonstrated successes and even fewer examples of how empowerment projects have fared compared with plausible alternatives. If policy and project responses cannot ultimately demonstrate their efficacy, they will not (and probably should not) be continued. This need not mean deferment to quantitative measures alone; it should mean putting considerable energies and resources into carefully designing an evaluation strategy that does the best it can to disentangle project from non-project effects. Similarly, improving the feedback loops from research and evaluation can ensure that projects themselves become both a beneficiary and source of information. Researchers and theorists have at least as much to gain from working alongside existing projects as do project task managers from attempting to keep up with the latest scholarly prognostications.

A Final Thought

This short paper has argued that an effective empowerment agenda will be one that takes seriously the tasks of collecting data, clarifying concepts, garnering political support, and evaluating projects. Though the spirit that informs much of the advocacy work on empowerment assumes that more empowerment is better, it is worth remembering that a host of studies in political sociology (Moore 1967) and economic history (Bates 2000) have shown that violence and prosperity go hand in hand; indeed, that revolutions are more likely to occur when conditions are getting better, not worse. The development community needs to recognize that by virtue of being in the poverty reduction business it is also, necessarily, in the revolutions business. Successfully empowering the poor is likely to lead to more, not less, conflict. I suggest that development strategies need to give equal attention to the conditions that support economic growth, social inclusion, and conflict mediation. A focus on empowerment should be part of, not a substitute for, such a strategy.

References

Barron, Patrick, Rachael Diprose, David Madden, Claire Q. Smith, and Michael Woolcock. 2004. Can participatory development projects help villagers manage local conflict? Assessing the Kecamatan development project, Indonesia. Working Paper No. 9 (Revised version), Conflict Prevention and Reconstruction Unit, Washington, DC: World Bank.

Bates, Robert. 2000. *Violence and prosperity*. New York: Norton.

Moore, Barrington. 1967. *The social origins of democracy and dictatorship*. Boston: Beacon.

Narayan, Deepa, ed. 2002. *Empowerment and poverty reduction: A sourcebook*. Washington, DC: World Bank.

Pritchett, Lant. 2002. It pays to be ignorant: A simple political economy of rigorous program evaluation. *Policy Reform* 5 (4): 251–69.

———. 2003. Who is not poor? Proposing a higher international standard for poverty. Mimeo, Harvard University, Kennedy School of Government.

Tilly, Charles. 1998. *Durable inequality*. Berkeley, CA: University of California Press.

Whiteside, Katherine, Michael Woolcock, and Xavier de Souza Briggs. 2004. Evaluating social development projects: Integrating the art of practice and the science of evaluation. Mimeo, Development Research Group, World Bank.

World Bank. 2000. *World development report 2000/2001: Attacking poverty*. New York: Oxford University Press.

Part II

Supplemental Materials

8. Measuring Empowerment: An Analytic Framework

Ruth Alsop, Nina Heinsohn, and Abigail Somma

Empowerment—the process of enhancing an individual's or group's capacity to make choices and transform those choices into desired actions and outcomes—is an increasingly familiar term within the World Bank. First given organizational recognition through the *World Development Report 2000-2001*, "empowerment" is now found in the documentation of over 1,800 World Bank-aided projects, and it is the subject of numerous learning activities. However, there is no consistent analytic framework to help those involved in analysis and lending activities structure their thinking about how to operationalize empowerment in various contexts, or how to track empowerment activities or effects. This note outlines such a framework.

The framework was developed as part of an ongoing study to identify indicators and instruments for measuring and tracking empowerment. Five country teams are engaged in testing the framework and developing context-specific indicators for a range of projects. These include the participatory budgeting initiative in Brazil, the Women's Development Initiatives Project in Ethiopia, the Community-Based Education Project in Honduras, the Kecamatan Development Project in Indonesia, and the Rural Water Supply and Sanitation Project in Nepal.[1]

---

1. To find out more about the cross-country study and individual projects, please visit the Empowerment Web site at www.worldbank.org/empowerment.

Concepts

If a person or group is empowered, they possess the capacity to make *effective* choices.   As Figure 1 indicates, we suggest that this capacity is influenced primarily by two inter-related factors: agency and opportunity structure. Agency is defined as an actor's ability to make meaningful choices; that is, the actor is able to envisage and purposively choose options.   Opportunity structure is defined as those aspects of the context within which actors operate that determine their ability to transform agency into effective action.   Working together, these factors give rise to different degrees of empowerment.[2]

FIGURE 1.   The Relationship between Outcomes and Correlates of Empowerment

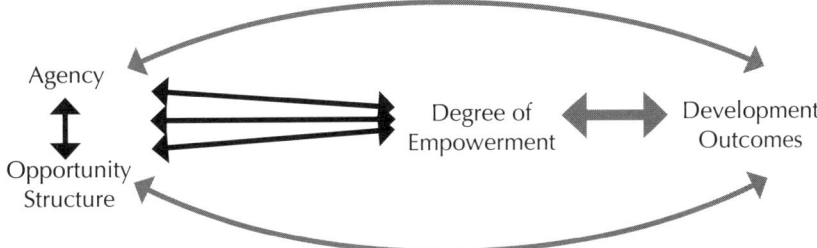

In the five-country study, a person's or group's *asset endowment* is used as an indicator of agency.   These assets include psychological, informational, organizational, material, financial, and human assets.

An actor's opportunity structure is shaped by the presence and operation of *formal and informal institutions*, which include the laws, regulatory frameworks, and norms governing people's behavior.

---

2. Earlier conceptualizations of this framework referred to four "forms of empowerment" (passive access, active participation, influence, and control).   Based on field experiences, this terminology has been superseded by the current identification and measurement of different "degrees of empowerment."   Figure 1 also indicates an assumed relationship between empowerment outcomes and development outcomes, albeit one that is mediated by a range of other influences.   While there is much scattered evidence suggesting this is true, the relationship is something that ongoing and proposed empirical work has yet to prove.

Measurement of assets and institutions provides intermediary indicators of empowerment. Direct measures of empowerment can be made by assessing:

(a) if an option exists to make choice,
(b) if the option to choose is used, and
(c) the result achieved if the choice is made.

To illustrate, if a team were trying to assess the degree of political empowerment of women, information would first need to be gathered on the existence of women's opportunities for political participation, such as the presence of a local elected body, whether elections are held, and whether any affirmative action policies exist. Then the question would be asked, do women *choose* to participate in the elected body, to vote, or to make use of the space opened up by a policy? Finally, the team would assess the outcome of choices; that is, do women *actually* participate, vote, or use opportunity?

Having no choice at all for a desired outcome can occur for many reasons, including geographic, social, or economic positioning of a person or group.

The relationship between agency, opportunity structure, and degree of empowerment is not simple, and it is rarely linear. In this framework, both agency and opportunity structure are treated as (1) causally related to the degree of empowerment of a group or individual, (2) contingent on a degree of empowerment, and (3) modifiable as a result of empowerment processes.

Context

In practice, agency, opportunity structure, and degrees of empowerment vary according to context. This context can be at the county level or at various levels within countries. People's capacity to make effective choices varies according to what they are doing and the level at which they are acting. An Indian woman will experience a different form of empowerment within the household when she is trying to exercise choice over domestic resources from that which she will experience in the office of a government bureaucrat when trying to use a government service, or when in a bank trying to access a loan. She will also have different experiences according to whether she is trying to operate in, for example, her village of residence, a market or office located at a distance from that village, or in a capital city. These added complexities in the measurment of empowerment are dealt with by conceptualizing three different domains and three different levels of actors' lives. This conceptualization is imporant to an analytic framework that has to span the multiple political, social, and economic conditions found in different countries.

A domain is an area of a person's life; it is a stage upon which specific roles are played out. The study posits three domains:

- the state, in which a person acts as a citizen,
- society, in which a person is a social actor, and
- the market, in which a person is an economic actor.

Each of these domains is divided into sub-domains. For example, justice and politics are sub-domains of the state; credit, labor, and goods are sub-domains of the market; and household and community are subdomains of society. These domains and sub-domains are those commonly experienced by citizens, albeit in different ways in different countries.

Analysis of one level of domain or sub-domain will not reflect the reality of most people's lives. Within countries, people behave in different ways and enjoy different forms of empowerment depending on the *level* at which they engage. These can minimally be identified as:

- the local level, which comprises the immediate vicinity of a person's everyday life. This is likely to be the level of community.
- the intermediary level, which comprises a vicinity which is familiar but which is not encroached upon on an everyday basis. This is likely to be the level between the community and national level.
- the macro-level, which comprises a vicinity which is the furthest away from the individual. This is likely to be the national level.

For example, in Ethiopia, the macro-level could correspond to the federal, the intermediary to the *woreda*, the micro, to the *kebele*, or village. In India, the macro-level might correspond to the state, the intermediary to the district, and the local to the panchayat.

The Framework in Practice

In summary, empowerment can be assessed at different *domains* of a person's life (the state, the market, society) and at different *levels* (macro, intermediary, and local). Each domain can be divided into sub-domains. At the intersect of a sub-domain and a level, people can experience different degrees of empowerment (existence of choice, use of choice, effectiveness of choice), answering the question, *How much/to what extent is a person empowered?* The degree of empowerment is contingent upon two clusters of interdependent factors: the agency of the actor and the opportunity structure within which that actor operates. The agency of an actor is largely determined by the actor's asset endowment. His or her opportunity structure is largely determined by the presence and operation of formal and informal institutions. Looking at how agency and opportunity structure affect the degree of empowerment sheds light upon the question *why* an actor is empowered in one way or another. Table 1 summarizes this approach to measuring empowerment.

As examples from the multi-country measuring empowerment study demonstrate, the application of this framework is not difficult. The focus of any

TABLE 1. **Summary of Analytic Framework**

DOMAIN		CONTRIBUTORY FACTOR	LEVEL		
	Sub-domain		Macro	Intermediary	Local
State	Justice	Agency (A)[1]	Degree of empowerment (DOE)[3]	DOE	DOE
		Opportunity Structure (OS)[2]			
	Politics	A	DOE	DOE	DOE
		OS			
	Service Delivery	A	DOE	DOE	DOE
		OS			
Market	Credit	A	DOE	DOE	DOE
		OS			
	Labor	A	DOE	DOE	DOE
		OS			
	Goods	A	DOE	DOE	DOE
		OS			
		OS			
Society	Household	A	DOE	DOE	DOE
		OS			
	Community	A	DOE	DOE	DOE
		OS			

[1] Agency is measured through endowment of psychological, informational, organizational, material, financial, and human assets.

[2] Opportunity Structure is measured through presence and operation of informal and formal rules.

[3] Degree of Empowerment is measured through existence of choice, exercising the opportunity to choose, and outcome of choice.

effort to measure and explain empowerment will, however, determine which indicators are chosen and where they are clustered.

In the first example, the Honduras case study examines whether the devolution of authority over schooling to community education councils leads to the empowerment of parents vis-à-vis school staff. Specifically, it assesses whether and to what extent parents have a say in school-related decision making. Indicators for this case cluster in the service delivery and community sub-domain, at the local level. Indicators of parents' degree of empowerment include, among others, their attendance at school council meetings and the ability to hold teachers accountable for their performance. Parents' awareness of their rights and responsibilities associated with joining the community school councils as well as prior participation in community matters are examples of asset indicators. Indicators of opportunity structure include, for instance, the existence and operation of rules that determine whether members of disadvantaged groups, including women, ethnic minorities, and the poor, can be involved in the community education councils.

In the Women's Development Initiative in Ethiopia, indicators cluster in the realm created at the intersect of the local level and the sub-domains of household, community, legal services, and goods. In this project, DOE indicators include women's ability to participate in or influence community meetings (community), to make intra-household consumption or investment decisions (household), and to access courts (legal services). The ratio of girls who are enrolled in and complete primary and secondary education constitutes an asset indicator. Finally, the existence and operation of norms and laws that discriminate against women are indicators of the opportunity structure.

Summary

This framework should provide a useful starting point for other researchers interested in tracking and measuring empowerment. It also provides a basic framework that can assist in identifying priority areas for future investments in empowerment. The ongoing multi-country study is expected to yield indicators, instruments, guidelines, and a cross-country paper in February 2005. As information and results become available, updates will be tracked on the empowerment Web site. For more information, please see: www.worldbank.org/empowerment.

9. Working Meeting on Power, Rights, and Poverty Reduction: A Summary

Nina Heinsohn

This paper summarizes the key points and issues raised during a two-day working meeting on power, rights, and poverty reduction, jointly hosted by the UK's Department for International Development (DFID) and the World Bank. The meeting allowed participants to take stock of different approaches to understanding the relationship between empowerment, power relations, rights, and poverty, and to identify opportunities to integrate this knowledge into the Bank's and DFID's work. Day one focused mainly on the conceptual and practical linkages between empowerment, power, rights, and poverty reduction. Day two centered on the questions of whether and how the two donor organizations could give their work programs a stronger focus on these issues, and which organizations they could collaborate with.

Addressing questions of empowerment, power relations, and rights is increasingly important to DFID's and the Bank's work on poverty reduction. The World Bank defines empowerment as increasing the capacity of individuals and groups to make choices and transform these choices into desired actions and outcomes. Central to this definition is the understanding that imbalances in power relations affect people's capacity to make effective choices and benefit from poverty reduction efforts. An empowerment approach has direct relevance to rights-based approaches to development, which, depending on one's perspective, are based on a sense of justice and equity in relations between people, as well as on the idea that individuals have a set of entitlements which the state is responsible to advance, promote, and protect.

The terms *empowerment* and *rights* are used frequently within the Bank and DFID. Yet, uncertainty remains over a number of issues relating to these terms, including:

- the differences or synergies between empowerment and rights-based approaches to development;
- the extent to which power relations, as central to a discussion on empowerment, should be addressed by DFID and the Bank; and
- the way in which addressing power relations, within the context of an empowerment agenda, might be translated into meaningful instruments and operational practices that further poverty alleviation practices.

These are the issues the meeting sought to address. The remainder of this summary draws out key points and themes highlighted during the presentations and subsequent plenary discussions. In part, the summaries also draw on the background papers that were commissioned for the meeting.[1]

Opening Remarks

In his opening remarks, Gobind Nankani, the Vice President of PREM Network, spoke of his own experiences as Country Director in Brazil, where it became very clear to him that empowerment was critical to development processes. He discussed the Bank's commitment to empowerment, stressing that the Bank is primarily interested in the instrumental value of empowerment, while recognizing that for many Bank staff and clients, empowerment also had high intrinsic value.

Nankani noted that concern about empowerment and rights issues extended beyond the PREM group and that the Bank has increasingly addressed empowerment across many networks and sectors since the *World Development Report 2000-2001*. However, Nakani said, there is further consolidation and substantive work to be done, and the Bank's Empowerment Community of Practice offers one way of building on experience to take these agendas forward.

---

1. The papers and presentations are available at www.worldbank.org/empowerment.

Nankani also recognized that empowerment and rights are of interest to other development organizations, and he thanked DFID for co-sponsoring the meeting, encouraging further interaction and collaboration between our two organizations and others. Mr. Nankani ended by suggesting that more could be done within and between agencies to further these key areas of development practice.

Session 1: Exploring the Concepts

Presentations by Rosalind Eyben (Institute of Development Studies) and Caroline Moser (International Food Policy Research Institute/Overseas Development Institute) aimed to highlight the different approaches to the concepts of power, empowerment, and rights.

In "Linking Power and Poverty Reduction" Eyben pointed out that power is a complex concept and that positionality—which includes personal identity, education, and life experiences—shapes the way each individual defines and thinks about power. She also suggested that while it would be important for the meeting participants to gain conceptual clarity over the term power, it would be impractical for them to seek agreement on a common definition. Eyben then introduced Foucault's idea of the inseparability of power and knowledge and explained that power and knowledge work through discourses that frame how we think and act. She then stressed the importance of deconstructing discourses to reveal the effects power relations have. Following this theoretical overview, Eyben used a power analysis to explain why a large number of Bolivians lack identity cards, the economic, social, and political ramifications of lacking an identity card, and how power structures were challenged to tackle this problem.

Moser's presentation on "Rights, Power, and Poverty Reduction" focused on the following four topics: (1) the background to a rights-based approach to development, (2) the adoption and adaptation of rights into international development debates and policies, (3) the implementation of rights-based approaches, and (4) top-down vs. bottom-up entry points for the contestation of rights. Moser stressed the overlaps between rights-based approaches and empowerment approaches to development by pointing out that they share similar normative principles, among them equality and non-discrimination, participation and inclusion, accountability, and the rule of law. Further overlaps are demonstrated by the Bank's implicit work on human rights. Moser also explained that analyzing and implementing rights-based approaches requires a strong focus on institutions as well as an understanding of how social and political processes and dynamics determine poor people's abilities to make claims. She concluded by arguing that, while top-down legal frameworks provide an important normative basis on which to claim rights, practice demonstrates that bottom-up mobilization and local advocacy campaigns might be necessary for the successful contestation of rights.

Following the two presentations, the floor was opened up to a plenary discussion, during which the following points were raised:

- There is a distinction and an interplay between formal and informal power structures;
- Client governments resist addressing power relations in their countries;
- There are successful examples of top-down approaches in bringing about change, for example, in South Asia;
- There is tension between individual empowerment and collective action, an issue around which a large part of the plenary discussion revolved;
- Eyben introduced a matrix for understanding the different underlying ideological approaches to well-being to reiterate her point that our ideological assumptions inform our personal and organizational approaches to empowerment.

Session 2: Exploring the Linkages in Practice

This session was based on the premise that, while rights and power are implicitly linked, the design of poverty reduction strategies and programs requires greater clarity over how they can be related in practice and how these linkages can be exploited for greater poverty alleviation impacts.

Andrew Norton (DFID) opened up the session, discussing the commonalities between empowerment approaches and rights-based approaches to development, the characteristics of rights-based approaches, and the incorporation of rights-based approaches into DFID's work. Regarding the commonalities between empowerment and rights-based approaches, Norton pointed out that both strategies focus on such issues as equity, social justice, and the multidimensionality of poverty. He then discussed the characteristics and focal areas of rights-based approaches, including the emphasis on systems of redress, the focus on relationships (between citizens and the state), the importance of accountability, and the need to analyze structures of power and authority to better understand patterns of exclusion and discrimination as well as links between formal and informal rules and norms.   Norton explained that DFID is incorporating rights-based approaches into its work through the following activities: knowledge development, the establishment of new policies, and country-level work.   However, he also commented that, although DFID has an explicit policy on human rights and development, DFID's primary framework of objectives does not have a strong rights focus.   Furthermore, DFID's work on poverty reduction strategies is only marginally influenced by ideas related to rights-based approaches.   Operationalizing a rights approach raises complex challenges, and DFID would not claim to have all the answers.

The subsequent plenary discussion revolved around the following issues:

- Some Bank activities already support the human rights agenda (for example, the Bank's policy on indigenous people);
- Bank staff face institutional barriers to pushing for a stronger inclusion of rights and empowerment into the Bank's work;
- The language on power, rights, and empowerment must be made intelligible to colleagues who are less familiar with social development issues ("technocratization" of language);
- What is the legitimate use of power, and what is the basis of legitimacy that allows donors to be involved in power structures and dynamics?

Session 3: Power and Poverty–Focusing on Key Issues

During this session, David Mosse (School of Oriental and African Studies) and Jonathan Fox (University of California, Santa Cruz) discussed why addressing power relations is critical to poverty reduction and which issues arise when formal and informal power structures intersect.   Mosse, in his presentation "Power Relations and Poverty Reduction," first discussed a series of theoretical issues related to the concepts of power, including the linkages between formal and informal power structures, finite vs. infinite definitions of power, and actor-oriented vs. structural views of power.   Mosse also highlighted a number of different approaches of empowerment as a means to poverty reduction that draw on different ideas of the concept of power.   Comparing the impacts of decentralization and poverty reduction programs in two Indian states, Mosse concluded by emphasizing the importance of wider political context—such as the political interests of governments in power and historically shaped statewide power structures—in determining empowerment and poverty outcomes.

Fox's presentation on "Empowerment and Institutional Change: Mapping 'Virtuous Circles' of State-Society Interaction," focused on the interaction between formal and informal power relations at the national and local levels during design and implementation of pro-poor reform initiatives.   He raised a series of conceptual issues, including (1) the differences and synergies between empowerment (referring to actors' capacities) and rights (referring to the nominal opportunity structure); (2) the effects of power struggles between pro- and anti-reformers within the state apparatus; and (3) the limitations of focusing solely on empowerment at the local level. He made the following key points: most people are not active agents all the time; there is an interactive and uneven dynamic between the creations of rights/entitlements and the effective use of these; and vulnerable people are less likely to be able to take advantage of opportunity structures than others. Fox then presented a comparison of Mexican rural development programs that institutionalize the participation of indigenous people's organizations in the public sector, demonstrating how the interplay of formal and informal power relations affect empowerment outcomes.

During the plenary discussion the following points were made:

- Development practitioners need to deepen their understanding of both the dynamics and uses of collective action as well as of how institutional change can be effectively achieved;
- There can be tension among practices that seek to change the status quo, often reflected in a passive resistance to furthering structural change and co-option of new systems/rules;
- In terms of furthering an empowerment agenda, there is value in working with multiple stakeholders who comprise both close and distant allies.

Session 4: Implications
During the last session of day one, participants split into three groups to discuss the implications of the previous sessions for the work of DFID and the Bank.

Specifically, groups were asked to discuss the following question: "Who do we need to work with—inside and outside of our organizations—on what sort of activities, using which kind of instrument?"

Group one focused on the actors DFID and the Bank could work with in pushing forward a stronger empowerment and rights agenda in their respective organizations. It was agreed that potential collaborators and target audiences would include external and internal stakeholders as well as traditional/visible and invisible actors. In terms of the Bank, the target audience would include the board of executive directors (taking into account that some developing countries are increasingly gaining voice). Country teams are also a target because they are most directly in contact with client governments. As to external collaborators or target audiences, group one agreed that client governments (including ministries that are traditionally less involved), NGOs, and civil society were important.

Group two identified three actors who are key to advancing the proposed agenda: skeptical colleagues within each institution, government clients, and local institutions. The primary mechanism identified for collaborating with these actors was analytic work. When working with internal colleagues, the group stressed the importance of developing ways to better measure empowerment, power, and rights, and their impacts to provide ways to tangibly grasp their importance. For government clients, the group suggested that analytic work on these issues could underpin the design and monitoring of interventions. The group also emphasized that working with local institutions would be critical, since local researchers and NGOs are better able to place analysis in its particular context. Finally, the group stressed that both the Bank and DFID must understand that they are perceived as having certain levels of power themselves.

Group three made similar recommendations, suggesting that the two organizations collaborate with wider constituencies (academic networks, foundations, human rights groups, and the like) while at the same time pushing for greater interdisciplinary work within their own organizations. The group also pointed out that a series of the Bank's analytic and operational instruments have been reformed to incorporate issues of participation, gender, and safeguards, and raised the question of how far similar achievements could be made with regards to power, empowerment, and rights. The group suggested that relevant actors seize strategic opportunities within the Bank to pilot innovative analytic and operational work, such as the integration of an empowerment component into poverty assessments.

Session 5: Approaches to Understanding the Linkages to Power and Poverty

The two panelists of this session, Jeremy Holland (University of Wales) and Michael Woolcock (World Bank), presented on measuring empowerment at the national and local levels, respectively. In his presentation "Measuring Empowerment: Country Indicators," Holland first stressed some of the inherent difficulties in measuring empowerment, among them the relational, intrinsic, and intangible nature of power; the context specificity of empowerment; and the dynamics and non-predictability of the way power relations play out in practice. First describing the analytic framework that the Bank's Empowerment Team developed for measuring empowerment, Holland then discussed intermediate as well as direct indicators of empowerment. Holland concluded by explaining that indicators of empowerment relate to a spectrum of concepts that range from awareness, inclusion, and influence to control.

Michael Woolcock discussed a series of issues that relate to measuring empowerment at the local level. Woolcock first explained that while the Bank has largely integrated such concepts as empowerment and exclusion into its discourse, analysis of these concepts is not yet at an advanced stage. As he pointed out, this is largely due to the deficiency of the Bank's standard data sources and techniques in capturing the processes and contexts that determine exclusion and disempowerment. He then suggested that the Bank should (1) expand and improve existing household sources on development outcomes and their determinants (to understand who is excluded from what), and (2) engage in more context- and issue-specific research using mixed-methods (to understand how and why certain groups are excluded). Woolcock also explained that policy and project responses to disempowerment need to be technically sound, politically supportable, and administratively implementable.

The following points were raised during the plenary discussion:

- It is important to examine not only empowerment and the powerless, but also structures and cohesion among the powerful;
- Donors should not keep information gained from monitoring and evaluation to themselves; rather, they should distribute it among the studied communities;
- When social development concepts are assessed econometrically, they gain legitimacy.

Session 6: What Is Currently Missing from Our Work?

In this session, Jennie Richmond (DFID) and Susan Wong (World Bank) discussed a series of entry points for integrating power and rights related analysis and operations into the two donor organizations' work. Richmond stressed that DFID and the Bank should make use of the lessons learned when other "concepts of change" (such as gender and poverty reduction) were introduced to the organizations' agendas. She suggested that DFID integrate rights and power into (1) its work at the country level, bearing in mind that donors themselves have substantial power even though they consider themselves neutral actors, (2) its research and analytic activities, for example by integrating a power analysis into its Poverty and Social Impact (PSIA) work, and (3) its program design.

Wong suggested similar areas of action, among them (1) analytic work and research (including PSIA, ethnographic work, quantitative/qualitative studies); (2) poverty research, including integrating more social and political variables in activities related to poverty mapping, poverty profiles, inequality, and power mapping, (3) policy work (PRSPs and CAS), and (4) project and sectoral work. She also pointed out the need to look at the funding side—at the moment the Bank relies heavily on Trust Funds to study such issues. Limited Bank funding is available, and little is available for contributions to mainstream ESW products.

Further issues that were raised during the group discussion include:

- Other stakeholders should be included in forwarding rights and power agendas, such as the UN, civil society, foundations, academic and research institutions, and other bilateral donor agencies;
- What terminology should be used when working on these issues: human rights, empowerment, or both?
- Does empowerment have intrinsic or instrumental value, or both?

Session 7: Implications for Work Programs and Collaboration

This session asked participants to divide into two groups to discuss work program implications for DFID and the Bank, respectively.

The DFID group (which included independent researchers and practitioners) suggested the establishment of a "community of practice" among organizations that work on related issues (such as donors, civil society, and academic institutions) to provide a platform for coordination and communication. In addition, the group identified possible areas of collaboration, including:

- joint reviews and country analyses;
- implementing a program around a headline initiative, such as how donors affect power relations and social exclusion; and
- working together in selected regions or countries to draw out positive or negative lessons.

Some participants from DFID indicated that they thought the analytic framework developed by PREM's Empowerment Team worked because its presentation is simple and its language is accessible.

In terms of work within the boundaries of its own institutions, DFID participants suggested working both at the country level as well as at its headquarters, integrating power and rights themes into its policy work and its activities on PSIA and exclusion.

The group representing World Bank staff first discussed examples of Bank activities that already address issues related to power and rights, such as previous and upcoming WDRs; the PREM Empowerment Team's work, including the study on Moving Out of Poverty; and the work carried out by the Bank's Governance and LICUS teams. The group highlighted the need to work on visible products as vehicles for carrying change forward.

The group considered collaboration with both external and internal actors important, as was the need to engage with local actors and bring in new partners. The group placed special emphasis on the need to avoid fragmentation among different Bank teams working on social development issues. The group also agreed that the work on power, empowerment, and rights should make use of existing instruments rather than lead to the creation of new instruments, and it identified PRSPs as a focal area of action. From the Bank's perspective, collaboration between agencies should focus on demonstrating the instrumental role empowerment plays in poverty reduction.

The group suggested that joint action could focus on:

- PRS monitoring systems and poverty analysis;
- analysis of the organizational mechanisms and processes used in existing projects or donor instruments to further an empowerment and rights approach to development.

Throughout this last session, participants stressed that donors will need to include their own role in any kind of power analysis and that the power and rights terminology needs to be made accessible to non-social scientists and to those not familiar with the issues.

10. Understanding the Concept of Power

Fruzsina Csaszar, World Bank

The concept of power is central to the study of many social sciences, including political science, sociology, political economy, political anthropology, and international relations. Power is a complex and multi-layered concept that lacks a universally accepted definition. Scholars disagree about whether power is conflictual or consensual and about how power is created. This paper will explore the key points of the debate on defining power. The first part will examine the definitions and theories of power by the main power theorists of the twentieth century, who interpret power as being exercised through either conflictual or consensual mechanisms. The second part will examine different typologies of power and the meaning of empowerment within them.

PART I: DEFINING POWER

Conflictual Power Theorists

Conflictual power theorists view power as something inherently negative and noxious: power prohibits, power makes a person do what he would not have done otherwise, or to act against his interests. Conflictual power theorists presuppose that power is a zero-sum game, and they seek to define power in this context.

Within the school of conflictual power, the work of theorists Robert Dahl, Peter Bachrach and Morton Baratz, and Steven Lukes dominate the field. Their ideas build on one another, creating what is called the "three-dimensional power debate."[1] This three-dimensional power debate, outlined below, provides the foundation for the main theories of power used in the political and social sciences.

Dahl: Power as Decision Making

Within Dahl's framework, A has power over B to the extent that A can get B to do something which B would not have done otherwise. Within this paradigm, power refers to the act of prevailing in decision making and is not to be equated with power resources, which are only potential power. Dahl notes that resources may or may not be mobilized in decision making. For example, one wealthy person may choose to collect paintings, while another may make political contributions—both may have equal resources, but only the latter is powerful because the resources are used in the political realm. Thus, while resources are a factor in determining power, they determine potential power, not the degree of power itself.

In his study of power in a community in New Haven, Connecticut, Dahl (1961) analyzed who initiated and who vetoed decisions in key issue areas (political nominations, public education, and urban renewal). He found that while there was an unequal distribution of resources in the community, there was no single elite entity that exercised power in all three of the main issue areas. Rather, there was a variety of competing power structures, none of which was dominant. From this he concluded that there was not one elite in New Haven, but a plurality of elites. Thus, Dahl argued that modern democracies deliver democratic outcomes through competition between elites, a form of government he termed "polyarchy."

Dahl's model of power was criticized by many, including Bachrach and Baratz and Lukes, who argued that his concept of power was too narrow. The following sections examine the theories of power that grew out of their elaborations on Dahl's definition of power.

Bachrach and Baratz: Power as Agenda Setting

Bachrach and Baratz add to Dahl's theory on power by emphasizing that not only does A exercise power over B in overt decision making, but A may also

---

1. Much of the analysis of power theorists in this paper is based on Mark Haugaard 2002.

exercise power over B by limiting the scope of the political decision making to an agenda determined by A.

Thus, Bachrach and Baratz (1962) add to Dahl's dimension of power as decision making by introducing a second "dimension" that takes into account the manner in which decisions are made and can be influenced. The clearest example of this is the process of agenda setting, where an issue of importance to B is deliberately left off the agenda by A. This form of power is called nondecision making; that is, the decision not to make a decision. This second dimension of power is exemplified by actions such as excluding items from an agenda, creating selective precedents, defining matters as a private affair, excluding others by endless red tape, creating committees that never reach decisions, or "losing" files.

What goes on in back rooms and unofficially at the level of local, national, and international politics are instances of two-dimensional power. However, many biases are not of this form, which is where Lukes enters the power debate.

Lukes: Power in Terms of Interests

Lukes (1974) introduces a third dimension of power by examining power in terms of interests: A exercises power over B when A affects B in a manner contrary to B's interests. Lukes criticizes the behavioral focus of both Dahl and Bachrach and Baratz. Instead of emphasizing the behavior of people in decision making, Lukes makes a more radical argument that power is formed by society. According to Lukes, biases are not necessarily reducible to the actions or deliberate non-actions of individuals, but rather they are inherited from the past in the form of structured or culturally patterned behavior of groups. The second aspect of Lukes' view on power is his emphasis on "false consciousness," a term Lukes uses to describe the prevailing social "ideology" in which the less powerful are not aware of their "real interests."

Central to Lukes' conceptualization of power is the relationship between power and knowledge. The underlying premise of the third dimension of power is that power distorts knowledge by warping or distorting the truth in a direction that is beneficial to the specific interests of the dominant group. While this concept of false consciousness lends itself to conspiracy theories and must be scrutinized, Lukes emphasizes that it is a mistake to overlook the relationship between social knowledge and power when analyzing power.

Consensual and "Middle-Ground" Power Theorists

Consensual power theorists believe that power is not necessarily linked with conflict, and that it does not have to be a zero-sum game. Instead, they argue that power is the capacity to achieve outcomes, whether these are achieved by force or benefit only certain sectors of society. Talcott Parsons is an example of a theorist who believes that power is mostly consensual. In the middle ground between the conflictual and consensual school are theorists such as Michel Foucault, Anthony Giddens, and Stewart Clegg, who argue that power is constituted by both conflict and consensus. The frameworks of these theorists are the most nuanced and complex of the main power theories.

Parsons: Power is Created and Legitimated by Society

Parsons' addition to the conceptualization of power is an important one because he draws attention to the generative aspects of social power that are ignored by conflictual power theorists. According to Parsons (1963), power is produced or created by society; thus, it can be expanded and it need not be a zero-sum game. Cutting a cake is zero-sum: the more cake one person gets, the less others have. However, Parsons believes power expands or contracts based on the amount of legitimate power available. It may be the case that a gain in power by some is not necessarily at the expense of others.

Parsons explains the production of power in terms of an analogy between the polity and the economy. The economy has a medium of money; the polity has the medium of power. The existence of money is based on a consensus on the value of money, which itself is an abstraction: money has value only because we believe that it does. Similarly, the power of those in authority is based on self-perpetuating beliefs in legitimacy. Parsons doesn't deny that some power relations are based on coercion or the threat of violence, but he perceives coercion as a poor substitute for consensual, legitimate power. Parsons argues that complex political systems rely on the legitimation of power as power is separated from its base of coercion. Power increases as legitimacy is gained through effectiveness, and it contracts when illegitimacy pervades the system because of the misuse of authority. For example, political regimes that coerce their populations generally do so because they lack the type of authoritative, legitimate power that Parsons has in mind when he defines "power."

This addition to the definition of power has several weaknesses. Parsons ignores conflictual power, and scholars have criticized his analogy between money and power for being too simplistic. Nevertheless, Parsons emphasizes some important points: power does not simply exist, it has to be created; the creation of power is related to the reproduction of social order; even if power is not always legitimate it is not equal to violence or coercion; power does not have to be a zero-sum game; and power is not inherently contradictory to the interests of the people.

Foucault: Power is Constituted by Free Subjects

Foucault (1980) insists that we must examine the relationship between power and consciousness. He argues that power has no essence; that is, power is not situated in any particular place. Therefore, Foucault asserts, power is not reducible to institutions such as government bodies. Instead, power is always relational (between people, between different departments within a ministry, etc.) and exists only when it is exercised. Secondly, Foucault believes that power is constituted or created in a network of relationships among subjects who are free to act.

The modern perception of the relationship between power and knowledge is a negative one in which power distorts the truth—the third dimension of power. Foucault calls this phenomenon "negative power" and distinguishes it from "positive power," which is the power to say yes and to produce new realities. Whereas Lukes assumed that there exists a knowledge that is free from power and thereby objective, Foucault believes that all knowledge is created by society and therefore cannot be objective.

For Foucault, power is not coercion or violence: violence takes place when the limits of power are reached. Foucault argues that conflict and war indicate an absence of a shared truth. In fact, he defines power as the "setting up of shared truths in order to avoid war." He characterizes power as a form of pacification that works by codifying and taming war through the imposition of socially constructed knowledge.

While Foucault does not articulate a comprehensive, coherent theory on power, his views of the social construction of power are an important addition to the power debate. Foucault's writings highlight the idea that the relationships between power and knowledge is not oppositional—it is mutually constitutive.

Giddens: Agency and Power

Giddens' analysis of power highlights the importance of agency and relies heavily on his theory of "structuration."[2] According to Giddens, agency is only possible because of resources that exist as a result of the meaning they are given by society. For example, the resources of a wealthy person or of a political leader exist only because of the meaning of money and authority.

Giddens (1984) believes that power is intrinsic to human agency. He believes that social actors are never completely governed by social forces. Even when they display outward compliance, people make rational assessments of any given situation and its viable alternatives; thus, compliance is a choice and does not automatically entail agreement. Giddens argues that the analysis of power entails uncovering the subtle mix of what actors do and refrain from doing, what they achieve and fail to achieve, and what they might have done but did not do. Giddens believes that power is enabling as well as constraining, and that power is exercised as a process. Power cannot be attributed to resources; rather, it is constituted through processes of negotiation between individuals in society.

Clegg: Frameworks or Circuits of Power

Clegg's description of power is a synthesis of several contemporary debates on power. He characterizes power in terms of the paradigm of Lukes and Giddens, and combines this with the "creation of meaning" analysis of Foucault. Clegg (1989) divides power into different circuits. Dahl's model of A exercising power over B is the first circuit of power—episodic power; that is, the power at the agency level, where agents are autonomous. This circuit is a reflection of a deeper, second circuit, dispositional power, which is where meanings are created, recreated, and contested. Because meanings are tied to rules, dispositional power is reflected in the "rules of the game" that constitute reality. While actors may resist meanings as single agents, the meanings themselves are

---

2. In brief, structuration was developed in response to the dualism that exists between subject-centered and object-centered social theories. Subject-centered theories place emphasis on individuals as creators of society, while objectivist theories focus on society itself and view agents as the effects of social order. Structuration attempts to bridge this divide by proposing that social structures exist as they are reproduced by agents, and agents define themselves as agents by reproducing social structures. The simultaneous moment of the reproduction of agency and structure is what is known as "structuration." Giddens argues that social structures give people a capacity for action as agents. Without the existence of social structures created by society, agents would not have the ability to act.

a reflection of a deeper systemic form. This deep, facilitative power is the third circuit of power, constituting the general systemic set of relations. This systemic circuit of power is comprised of systems of rewards and punishments, and it defines power and powerlessness at the macro-level.

According to Clegg, power is essentially paradoxical. The power of an agent is increased by the agent delegating authority; the delegation of authority can only proceed by rules; rules entail discretion; and discretion potentially empowers delegates. Thus, there is a form of hidden power within the rules, which can alter the very opportunity structure they constitute. This give-and-take in power relations produces the basis of "organizationally negotiated order."

Conclusion

That the concept of power cannot be encapsulated in one theoretical framework reflects its complexity. Indeed, power is multi-layered: it is a capacity, a relational phenomenon, and a structural phenomenon. While there is no coherent, universally accepted definition of power, this paper has outlined the two main theoretical camps of the power debate: the conflictual and consensual power theories.

Several of the power theorists mentioned above examine the relationship between the agent and society, the resulting legitimacy of power (or lack thereof), and the possibility for change and empowerment. This link between power and empowerment will be explored in the second part of this paper in order to make a connection between the theoretical notions of power and the practical ways in which power relations can be altered.

PART II. A TYPOLOGY OF POWER

Main Typologies of Power

As evidenced by the different theories of power outlined above, power is difficult to define because it is multidimensional and dynamic, changing according to context, circumstances, and interest. Power is an individual and collective force that can either undermine or empower citizens and their organizations. The typologies outlined below will examine the diverse expressions of power and explore the ways in which empowerment can occur, given these different expressions.[3]

---

3. This typology is widely referenced in empowerment literature. This paper relies on the work of Rowlands (1997) and Hughes (2003).

Power Over

This type of power can be characterized as controlling power, which may be met with compliance, resistance, or manipulation. This is the type of power most often debated in the political science/sociological literature. The three dimensions of power all seek to characterize this type of controlling power in order to find the root cause of the methods of control and the relationship between knowledge and power.

Power over has many negative manifestations, including repression, force, coercion, discrimination, corruption, and abuse. This type of power is seen as a zero-sum game: having power involves taking it from someone else and then using it to dominate others and prevent them from gaining it. In politics, those who control resources and decision making have power over those without such control.

In terms of power over, empowerment is concerned with bringing people who are outside of the decision-making process into it.

Power With

This is collaborative power, or having a sense of the whole being greater than the sum of the individuals, especially when a group tackles problems together. This type of power involves finding common ground among different interests and building collective strength. This type of power, along with the next two types, fall under the "positive power" category established by Foucault. Because it is based on mutual support, solidarity, and collaboration, *power with* multiplies individual talents and knowledge. This type of power can help bridge different interests, transform or reduce social conflicts, and promote more equitable relations.

Power To

This type of power refers to the potential of every person to shape his or her life and world. *Power to* is generative or productive power that creates new possibilities and actions without domination. It is expressed by people's ability to recognize their interests and to realize that they have the power to shape their circumstances to achieve a situation that is more favorable to their interests. Both *power to* and *power with* involve Lukes' definition of actors' "true interests."

In the realms of both *power to* and *power with*, empowerment is concerned with the processes by which people become aware of their own interests. This occurs relationally as people develop the ability to negotiate and influence the nature of a relationship and the decisions made within it.   In addition, empowerment can take place collectively, with the development of cooperation between individuals and collective action, enabling individuals to achieve more than each could achieve alone.

Power Within

This type of power concerns a person's sense of self-worth and self-knowledge. It is the capacity to imagine and to have hope, to believe that one is strong enough and has the right to change one's circumstances.   This is the least-mentioned type of power in power literature, perhaps because it is difficult to identify and measure.   Nevertheless, this type of personal power for self-actualization is an important component of the exercise of power.   *Power within* can be characterized as the spiritual strength that resides in each of us and makes us truly human.   Its basis is self-acceptance and self-respect, which extend to respect for and acceptance of others as equals.

In terms of this typology of power, empowerment is more than participation in decision making, it must also include the processes that lead people to perceive themselves as able to and entitled to make decisions. Many grassroots organizations focus on power within to help people affirm their personal worth and to recognize their power to and power with. The combination of these three forms of positive power is agency: the ability to act and to change one's world. This type of empowerment takes place mostly in the personal sphere, where a person develops a sense of self, individual confidence, and capacity.

Conclusion

Keeping in mind the multi-layered, multidimensional definitions of power outlined in the first part of this paper, empowerment emerges as a complex process of raising individual and collective consciousness, identifying areas of desired change, and making change happen.   The meaning of empowerment varies according to context and according to who is doing the measuring. As Ruth Alsop, Nina Heinsohn, and Abigail Somma explain in *Measuring Empowerment: An Analytic Framework* (2002), empowerment may be influenced in various ways by the agency of the actor, the opportunity structure within which the actor operates, and the form of empowerment that takes place. It is important to note that, as Jo Rowlands points out, "true power cannot be bestowed: it comes from within. Any notion of empowerment being 'given' by one group to another hides an attempt to keep control" (1997, 16). Indeed, Rowlands warns outside professionals to be clear that any *power over* they have in relation to the people they work with is likely to be challenged. Thus, a study of the different definitions and aspects of power is very important in development agencies' search to understand the complex nature of power so that these agencies can use their power in a manner that truly empowers people.

References

Alsop, Ruth, Nina Heinsohn, and Abigail Somma. 2002. Draft. Measuring empowerment: An analytic framework. Washington, DC: World Bank.

Bachrach, Peter and Morton Baratz. 1962. The two faces of power. *American Political Science Review* 56: 947–52.

Clegg, Stewart. 1989. *Frameworks of power*. London: Sage Publications.

Dahl, Robert. 1961. *Who governs? Democracy and power in an American city*. New Haven, CT: Yale University Press.

Foucault, Michel. 1980. *Power/knowledge: Selected interviews and other writings 1972–1977*. Trans and ed. Colin Gordon, Brighton, UK: Harvester Press.

Giddens, Anthony. 1984. *The constitution of society: Outline of the theory of structuration*. Cambridge, UK: Polity Press.

Haugaard, Mark. 2002. *Power: A reader*. Manchester, UK: Manchester University Press.

Hughes, Alexandra, and Joanna Wheeler, with Rosalind Eyben and Patta Scott-Villiers. 2003. Rights and Power Workshop: Report. Brighton, UK: Institute of Development Studies.

Lukes, Steven. 1974. *Power: A radical view*. London: Macmillan.

Parsons, Talcott. 1963. On the concept of political power. *Proceedings of the American Philosophical Society*, 107 (3): 232–63.

Rowlands, Jo. 1997. *Questioning empowerment: Working with women in Honduras*. Oxford, UK: Oxfam Publications.

11. Literature Review

Fruzsina Csaszar, World Bank

Arendt, Hannah. 1970. *On Violence*. New York: Harcourt, Brace & World.
Arendt explores the difference between violence in the hands of the state versus violence in the hands of extremist groups or individuals. She examines how terrorism is different from totalitarianism. She reasons that violence is the lack of access to power. Her thesis is that where there is lack of power or where power is slipping away, there is greater potential for violence: lack of power begets violence.

Bachrach, Peter and Morton Baratz. 1962. "The Two Faces of Power." *American Political Science Review* 56: 947–52.
Bachrach and Baratz argue that power is exercised not only through overt decision making but also through the mobilization of bias within the decision-making system. What counts as a key issue for decision makers can, in itself, be the consequence of power conflict. They argue that power is exercised not only by prevailing in a certain issue area, but may equally be exercised by organizing issue areas in and out of politics (that is, agenda setting). They also introduce a form of power called nondecision making. Nondecision making involves observable conflict, but it is not conflict that is visible inside the decision-making process.

Barnes, Barry. 1988. *The Nature of Power*. Cambridge: Polity Press.
Barnes argues that power denotes capacity. He distinguishes between natural power, which is derived from natural material objects, and social power, which is

derived from the agency of other members of society. Barnes argues that power is a capacity for action that actors gain through membership in a social system, and this membership gives them access to the use of power which the society produces. According to Barnes, the empowered actor may use the power which he or she has been delegated to act against the interests of the empowering power-holder. To guarantee that this does not happen, the power-holders must ensure that the power which they pass on is potentially recoverable.

Bernhagen, Patrick. 2002. *Power: Making Sense of an Elusive Concept.* **Dublin: Trinity College.**
This paper outlines the main dimensions of power as presented by Dahl, Bachrach and Baratz, and Lukes, and highlights some of the conceptual difficulties of Lukes' theory. Bernhagen argues that the third dimension of power, as posited by Lukes, is a restriction on human agency induced by the bias of the political system, and thus should be categorized under the heading of "structural dominance," not as a "dimension of power." In essence, Mernhagen argues that there are two effective dimensions of power, not three.

Bourdieu, Pierre. 1989. "Social Space and Symbolic Power." *Sociological Theory* **7 (1): 14–25.**
This essay focuses on the complicated interaction between objective social relations and the structures according to which people imagine and inhabit social space. After setting up the classic division between objectivism and subjectivism, Bourdieu posits a dialectical relationship between social structures and their representations. Basically, Bourdieu examines the ways in which people interact, the power of symbols in their interactions, and the ways in which leaders emerge to speak for an entire group. His sociological examination of bureaucratic group structures and the monopolization of power by individuals within such groups is an important addition to the study of power in professional behavior.

Clegg, Stewart. 1989. *Frameworks of Power.* **London: Sage Publications.**
This book explores the debate about power in modern society. Clegg argues that organization provides the "framework of power," and without knowledge of this framework, power cannot be adequately conceptualized. Clegg provides a comprehensive account of the different approaches to understanding power and presents a fresh synthesis, including his model of the "circuits of power."

This model traces the movement of power through three levels: at the micro level there is the "episodic circuit" (the day-to-day interaction of people through everyday power struggles); the middle level contains the "dispositional circuit" (where rules are constructed and reconstructed at the social level, and where authority is legitimated); and finally at the macro level is the "facilitative circuit." By categorizing the different interactions of power relations in such circuits, Clegg creates a useful model to inspect the machinery and workings of power.

Dahl, Robert. 1961. *Who Governs? Democracy and Power in an American City*. New Haven, CT: Yale University Press.
Within Dahl's framework, A has power over B to the extent to which A can get B to do something which B would not have done otherwise. In this paradigm, power refers to the act of prevailing in decision making and is not to be equated with power resources, which are only potential power. Dahl argues that modern democracies deliver democratic outcomes through competition between elites, a form of government he terms "polyarchy." Dahl's view of power as decision making constitutes what is commonly known as the "first dimension" of power.

Dowding, Keith. 1996. *Power*. Minneapolis: University of Minnesota Press.
Dowding makes a distinction between power and luck and develops the concept of systematic luck. He explains how some groups get what they want without trying, while the efforts of others are not rewarded. He discusses the "who benefits?" test, arguing that it cannot reveal who has power because many benefit through luck and others are systematically lucky. Dowding does not simply put forward theoretical arguments, he uses relevant concepts to illustrate and explain the debates on power at both the national and the local level.

Foucault, Michel. 1980. *Power/Knowledge: Selected Interviews and Other Writings 1972–1977*. Trans. and ed. Colin Gordon. Brighton, UK: Harvester Press.
Foucault argues that power has no essence; it is not situated in any particular place, and thus is not reducible to institutions. Instead, power is always power *exercised*. According to Foucault, power is located at the levels of struggle,

truth production, and knowledge. The common view of power is as something inherently negative and noxious: power prohibits and says no. Foucault calls this "negative power" and distinguishes it from "positive power," which is the power to say yes and to produce new realities. For Foucault, power is not violence— violence takes place where the limits of power are reached. War presupposes an absence of a shared truth, while power is the setting up of shared truths in order to avoid war. While Foucault does not articulate a comprehensive, coherent theory on power, his views of the social construction of power are an important addition to the power debate. Foucault's writings highlight the idea that the relationships between power and knowledge is not oppositional—it is mutually constitutive.

Gaventa, John. 1982. *Power and Powerlessness: Quiescence and Rebellion in an Appalachian Valley.* **Chicago: University of Illinois Press.**
Gaventa examines our understanding of power and powerlessness, social complacency, and rebellion. He illustrates his points with several empirical case studies of situations in which power was challenged in Appalachia. Gaventa explores the lack of political response from deprived people as a function of power relationships, and he illustrates how power works to develop and maintain the quiescence of the powerless. He also explores how rebellion alters power relationships. Gaventa examines the resistance of miners to a reform movement within the United Mine Workers of America. He asks why so many people opposed the reforms despite widespread corruption and autocracy within the union, and uses the study to illustrate how power may serve to protect the powerholder, by shaping the perceptions of the powerless and taking away the sense of their right to act.

Giddens, Anthony. 1984. *The Constitution of Society: Outline of the Theory of Structuration.* **Cambridge, UK: Polity Press.**
In this book, Giddens explores why societies are the way they are, and the ways in which actors create society. Giddens seeks an answer to the question of whether society constitutes actors or actors constitute society. He proposes that social structures exist in the moment they are reproduced by agents, and agents define themselves as agents by reproducing social structures. This simultaneous moment of the reproduction of agency and structure is what is known as "structuration." Giddens argues that social structures give us a capacity for

action as agents. Without the existence of social structures created by society, agents would not have the ability to act. Through his theory of structuration, Giddens makes it possible to discuss the links between, as well as within, these two analytical parts.

Gledhill, John. 1994. *Power and Its Disguises: Anthropological Perspectives on Politics*. London and Boulder, CO: Pluto Press.
Gledhill explores the complexities of local situations and the power relations that shape the global order. The book begins by analyzing the politics of societies such as indigenous states and non-Western agrarian civilizations in order to outline the politics of domination and resistance within the colonial contexts. Gledhill also examines the contemporary politics of Africa, Asia, and Latin America, showing that historically informed anthropological perspectives can contribute to debates about democratization by incorporating a "view from below" and revealing forces that shape power relations behind the formal facade of state institutions. Gledhill shows how the study of micro-dynamics of power in everyday life, coupled with sensitivity to the interactions between the local and global, can offer critical insights into the potential of social movements and the politics of rights, gender, and culture.

Goverde, Henri, et al., eds. 2000. *Power in Contemporary Politics: Theories, Practices, Globalizations*. London: Sage Publications.
This book provides an overview of the contemporary theory and practice of power in politics. Goverde introduces the concept of political power in a three-part framework: contemporary theories of power; applications of power processes and practices; and the implications of modern power flowing across the globe. The book explores the many structures of power in the contemporary world: theories of its construction and use; its operation in policy networks and its wider exercise at different levels in the political process; and structures of power from the local to the global. Among the many themes explored are the reproduction and the legitimization of power, the dynamics of resistance and coercion, the concepts of private and public power, and the impact of globalization processes and subsequent shifting power arrangements. Because it combines diverse perspectives and different tools of analysis, this is a comprehensive book on political power.

Hartsock, Nancy. 1998. *The Feminist Standpoint Revisited and Other Essays.* **Boulder, CO: Westview Press.**

Hartsock examines the development of theory within feminist communities in response to current concerns about representation and social change. Two central contentions shape this collection of essays: First, theory plays an important part in political action for social change. Second, political theorists must respond to and concentrate their energies on problems of political action, most fruitfully as these problems emerge in the context of efforts for social change. For Hartsock, the central theme within theory and political action is power and its relationship to epistemology. This collection of essays examines the role of feminism in power relations in the work place, seeks to redefine work, and examines the feminist movement and its interpretation of power and politics.

Hayward, Clarissa. 2000. *De-Facing Power.* **New York: Cambridge University Press.**

Hayward challenges the prevailing view of power as something powerful people have and use. Rather than seeing power as having a "face," she argues that power is a complex network of social boundaries—norms, identities, institutions—that define individual freedom for the "powerful" and "powerless" alike. The book's argument is supported by a comparative analysis of relationships within two ethnically diverse educational settings: a low-income, predominantly African-American urban school; and an affluent, predominantly white, suburban school.

Haugaard, Mark. 1992. *Structures, Restructuration, and Social Power.* **Aldershot, UK: Ashgate Publishing.**

In this work, Haugaard outlines three main ideas of power: the mainstream conflictual versus consensual theories of power; Giddens' theory of structuration; and his own theory that goes beyond Giddens by discussing destructuration and restructuration; that is, the taking apart and recreating of the structuration process of meaning and power, as described in Giddens' work (see above).

———. 1997. *The Constitution of Power.* **Manchester, UK, and New York: Manchester University Press.**

This is an excellent introduction to the main theories of power. Haugaard explains the views of power theorists Barnes, Lukes, Foucault, Giddens, and

Bachrach and Baratz. He also focuses on the ways in which these theories of power can be applied to areas such as conflict and consensus, freedom and constraint, and resources and capital.

———. 2002. *Power: A Reader*. **Manchester, UK, and New York: Manchester University Press.**
This volume is an essential introduction to different views on power. Haugaard presents the ideas of fifteen main theorists on power and follows each explanation of their theories with excerpts from their original texts.

Hindess, Barry. 1996. *Discourses of Power: From Hobbes to Foucault.* **Oxford, UK and Cambridge, MA: Blackwell Publishers.**
Hindess unravels the confusion of "power as capacity" and "power as right," which has been a problem in modern political theory from Hobbes and Locke. Hindess argues that Foucault's theories on power are squarely in the mainstream of modern political thought.   Hindess demonstrates the importance of Foucault's attempts to refocus the analysis of power onto the nature and forms of government. The book sums up both the strengths and limits of Foucault's challenge to political theory, and points out that assumptions about political communities as constraints on political thought still need to be critically examined.

Hughes, Alexandra, and Joanna Wheeler, with Rosalind Eyben and Patta Scott-Villiers. 2003. *Rights and Power Workshop Report.* **Brighton, UK: Institute of Development Studies.**
This workshop report examines the challenges to implementing rights-based approaches by highlighting issues of legitimacy of action, the practice of power, and the lines of accountability. The report outlines the main definitions of power and refers to John Gaventa's analysis of several types of power, including "visible power" (in open, public spaces); "hidden power" (the upholding of existing power dynamics that were established by a history of force and discretionary resource distribution); and "invisible/intangible power" (an internalized sense of power or powerlessness). The report emphasizes that power is dynamic, since each dimension of power is constantly changing and is interrelated with other power dimensions.

Kearnis, Kate. 1996. "Power in Organisational Analysis: Delineating and Contrasting a Foucauldian Perspective." *Electronic Journal of Radical Organisation Theory* 2 (2). University of Waikato, New Zealand.

This paper examines the main assumptions implicit in the predominant conceptions of power in organizational analysis. The paper discusses how a Foucauldian approach to power and power relations differs from more mainstream conceptions rooted in functionalist/behaviorist beliefs and radical structuralism. It highlights the role of Foucault's perspective on power in gaining a historical understanding of how power is exercised in organizations, and examines the effects of structuration in producing and maintaining power.

Lukes, Steven. 1974. *Power: A Radical View.* **London: Macmillan.**

Lukes argues that bias within a system is not sustained simply by a series of individually chosen acts, but also by the socially structured and culturally patterned behavior of groups and practices of institutions, which may be manifest by an individual's inaction. Lukes introduces interests into the concept of power: A exercises power over B when A affects B in a manner contrary to B's interests. The underlying premise of Lukes' conception of power is that power distorts knowledge by warping or distorting the truth in a direction that is beneficial to the specific interests of the dominant group. Lukes' theory of power is often characterized as the "third dimension" of power, relating to Dahl's first dimension and Bachrach and Baratz's second dimension.

Nelson, Nici and Susan Wright, eds. 1995. *Power and Participatory Development: Theory and Practice.* **London: Intermediate Technology Development Group Publishing.**

This book outlines the main types and dimensions of power and explores ways that development agencies can intervene in communities to encourage generative power. Nici and Wright examine the shifts in power that are needed for participatory ideas to be effective. With the goal of connecting theory and practice, the book outlines the theoretical basis to participatory development work and uses case studies to show that these basic ideas are applicable in different world regions. Finally, this book examines the changes needed for development institutions to operate in a truly participatory manner that empowers local communities.

Parsons, Talcott. 1963. "On the Concept of Political Power." *Proceedings of the American Philosophical Society* **107 (3): 232–63.**
Parsons' addition to the conceptualization of power is an important one because he draws attention to the generative aspects of social power that were ignored by conflictual power theorists. According to Parsons, power is not a zero-sum game, which is a perception of power based on the assumption that power is simply given. Parsons argues that power doesn't just exist—it has to be created. Power is produced or created by society; if it can be expanded then it is not a zero-sum game. Parsons argues that complex political systems rely on the legitimation of power as power is separated from its base of coercion. Power increases as legitimacy is gained through effectiveness, and it contracts when illegitimacy pervades the system because of the misuse of authority.

Polsby, Nelson. 1960. "How to Study Community Power: The Pluralist Alternative." *The Journal of Politics* **22 (3): 474–84.**
Polsby contrasts the pluralist approach to power, which states that nothing categorical can be assumed about power in any community, with the stratification approach, which states that some group necessarily dominates a community. Polsby highlights the main differences between the two schools of thought with respect to their conceptions on what is meant by power. Stratification theorists emphasize the cataloging of power bases (that is, the resources available to actors for the exercise of power), whereas pluralists concentrate on the exercise of power itself. This article is an important addition to power literature as it outlines the main points of study and methodologies that power researchers should use to conduct an effective study of power in communities.

Rowlands, Jo. 1997. *Questioning Empowerment: Working with Women in Honduras.* **Oxford, UK: Oxfam Publications.**
In her presentation of different definitions of empowerment, Rowlands examines the four main forms of power: *power over*, which is controlling power; *power to*, generative or productive power; *power with*, cooperation and teamwork where the whole is greater than the sum; and *power from within*, spiritual strength that is the basis for self-acceptance, self-respect, and respect for others. Using the conventional definition of *power over*, empowerment means bringing people who are outside the decision-making process into it. Within the framework of *power to*, empowerment is concerned with the processes by which people

become aware of their own interests and how those relate to the interests of others. Rowlands outlines three realms where empowerment can occur: the personal, the relational, and the collective.

Russell, Bertrand. 1938 (2004). *Power: A New Social Analysis.* **New York: Routledge.**

This book is primarily concerned with the classification of different sources of power, such as priestly, kingly, revolutionary, or economic. Russell's aim is to investigate how we can enjoy the advantages of state power and prevent the Hobbesian war of all against all, while taming state excesses. Power, he argues, is an ultimate human goal and the single most important element in the development of any society. He also examines the effectiveness of ideas and moral codes in buttressing or undermining power. Countering the totalitarian desire to dominate, Russell concludes by emphasizing that only political enlightenment and human understanding can lead to peace.

Tilly, Charles. 1998. *Durable Inequality.* **Berkeley: University of California Press.**

This work explores the reasons behind organizational inequality-producing mechanisms. According to Tilly, people establish systems of inequality mainly through four main mechanisms: *exploitation,* whereby the powerful command resources and draw increased returns by excluding outsiders; *opportunity hoarding,* whereby members of a network acquire access to a valuable, renewable resource that they can monopolize, increasing the network's power; *emulation,* the copying of established organizational models or social relations from one setting to another; and *adaptation,* the explanation of daily routines, such as political influence, on the basis of unequal structures. Tilly examines categorical identities and their role in politics, and considers the implications of the argument for deliberate intervention to change inequality.

VeneKlasen, Lisa, and Valerie Miller 2002. *A New Weave of Power, People, and Politics: The Action Guide for Advocacy and Citizen Participation.* **Oklahoma City: World Neighbors.**

This field manual provides an approach for promoting citizen participation. Its chapter on Power and Empowerment examines different aspects of power and suggests exercises for development practitioners to help empower people. This chapter also deals with different levels of political power, such as visible power (observable decision making, as described by Dahl), hidden power (setting the political agenda, as described by Bachrach and Baratz), and invisible power (shaping meaning, as described by Lukes, Foucault, and others). This chapter offers a concise, practically oriented introduction to power and empowerment concepts.